THE DONS' QUIZ BOOK

THE DONS' QUIZ BOOK

COMPILED BY **ALLY WALKER**

MAINSTREAM
PUBLISHING

First published in 1986 by
MAINSTREAM PUBLISHING COMPANY (EDINBURGH) LTD.
7 Albany Street
Edinburgh EH1 3UG

ISBN 1 85158 044 1

Walker, Ally
    The Dons' quiz book.
    1. Aberdeen Football Club——Miscellanea
    I. Title
    796.334′63′0941235   GV943.A233

    ISBN 1-85158-044-1

Typeset in 10/12 point Garamond.
Printed in Great Britain by Collins, Glasgow.

Contents

Introduction 7

Questions 11

Crossword 1 46

Crossword 2 50

Answers 99

Picture Quiz Answers 141

Diary 143

Now You Know 176

Introduction

Perhaps this quiz book all about "The Dons" will start more arguments than it will settle. Hopefully, however, you may find out something about Aberdeen Football Club that you never knew. Some questions you may be able to answer off the top of your head, others you may have to do some research in order to find out the answers. Of course you could also cheat and look up the answers at the back of this book!

I have on purpose jumbled up all the questions in preference to putting them into specific categories. This way, no matter what age group you belong to, you should still be able to answer at least some of them.

While carrying out the research for this book, I was somewhat surprised at just how little I knew about "The Dons", not only of the past but also of more recent times. In a way I was disappointed when the project ended as it becomes somewhat addictive searching through various snippets of news, especially if it is of a local nature. I hope you, the reader, will get as much satisfaction in trying to answer the questions as I had in their compilation.

I am sure you will find some of the questions easy, some a bit harder, some proper stinkers. Some you may have the answers to on the tip of your tongue, but try as you may it escapes you at the time; others, you will no doubt want to kick yourself for when you hear the answer.

ALLY WALKER

THE DONS' QUIZ BOOK

Questions

Quiz 1
Questions 1-20

1. Can you name the player Aberdeen transferred to Leeds United in July 1977?

2. Can you name the Aberdeen player who was named Scotland's Player of the Year in 1972?

3. How often have Aberdeen won the Drybrough Cup?

4. What is the record victory of the Dons?

5. What was the occasion when the Dons recorded their record victory?

6. Which Aberdeen player became the first Scottish player to score direct from a corner in an international match?

7. In the semi-final of the 1953/54 Scottish Cup Aberdeen beat their opponents 6-0. Who were their opponents?

8. Before joining the Dons, for which club did Doug Rougvie play?

9. In what year did Aberdeen avoid relegation by the narrowest of margins—but went on to win the League Cup a few months later?

10. On how many occasions have Aberdeen appeared in a Scottish Cup final, up to and including season 1985/86?

11. What was the nickname given to Arthur Graham while at Pittodrie?

12. What is the present-day capacity of Pittodrie—1986?

13. Have Aberdeen ever finished bottom of the old Scottish League Division One?

14. In what year did Aberdeen first appear in a semi-final of the Scottish Cup?

15. In what year did Albion Rovers knock Aberdeen out of the Scottish Cup?

16. Before joining Aberdeen, for which club did Ian Scanlon play?

17. In what year did Doug Rougvie join the Dons?

18. In what year did Ian Scanlon join the Dons?

19. Can you name the only Aberdeen-born and bred player in the

Dons' European Cup Winners Cup side 1983, who also played in the final?

20. How many consecutive games did Aberdeen play in season 1970-71 without conceding a goal?

Quiz 2
Questions 21-40

21. Between 1976 and 1980 how many times did Aberdeen appear in the finals of the League Cup?

22. Can you name at least five players in the Aberdeen Cup-winning side of 1970?

23. What was the approximate attendance at the Scottish Cup final, season 1953/54?

24. Name the scorer(s) of Aberdeen's goal(s) in the 1969/70 Scottish Cup final.

25. Aberdeen have appeared in the final of the Drybrough Cup on two occasions. Who were their opponents?

26. What is the record amount of league goals Aberdeen has scored in any one season?

27. What is the meaning of Pittodrie?

28. Have Wales ever played a full international match at Pittodrie?

29. In what season(s) have Aberdeen won the Drybrough Cup?

30. Can you name the stadium where Aberdeen appeared in the final of the European Cup Winners Cup 1983?

31. In what year was Aberdeen Football Club founded?

32. Who were Aberdeen's opponents in the 1976/77 League Cup final?

33. In what year did Aberdeen first win the Scottish Cup?

34. For which club did Dom Sullivan play before signing for the Dons?

35. Who were Aberdeen's opponents in the Scottish Cup final of 1947?

36. What is the record attendance at Pittodrie?

37. Can you name at least five players in Aberdeen's first-ever team to play in a European competition?

38. Who scored the winning goal in the League Cup final of 1976/77?

39. What was Aberdeen's highest win in the League in season 1979/80?

40. How often have Aberdeen won the Scottish Cup up to, and including, season 1985/86?

Quiz 3
Questions 41-60

41. A new record was created in the Scottish Cup 3rd round on 3 February 1973, Brechin v Aberdeen. What record was created?

42. In what years have Aberdeen won the Scottish Cup, up to season 1985/86?

43. Have Aberdeen ever played in the old Scottish League Division Two?

44. Can you name the player Aberdeen transferred to Liverpool in 1965?

45. Can you name at least five players in the Aberdeen team which played in the final of the Scottish Cup, season 1946/47?

46. In what season did Aberdeen first compete in a European competition?

47. What was the score in Aberdeen's first game in a European competition?

48. Can you name the Dons' top goal scorer in season 1979/80?

49. Apart from the European song, can you name three other records which have sung the praises of the Dons?

50. What stage did Aberdeen reach in the Scottish Cup in season 1972/73?

51. Who was the Dons' manager when Aberdeen won the League Cup in 1976/77?

52. While manager of the Dons, Ally McLeod signed five players. Can you name them?

53. From what club did Aberdeen buy Stuart Kennedy?

54. In the 1980/81 European Cup, Aberdeen v Austria Memphis, at Pittodrie, who scored Aberdeen's goal(s)?

55. In which season did Aberdeen first become League champions?

56. Although a signed Dons' player, Willie Miller was on loan to which Highland League club?

57. In what year, and against which country, did Willie Miller get his first full international cap?

58. Who scored Aberdeen's winning goal in 1946/47 Scottish Cup final?

59. Who were the last team to win the Drybrough Cup?

60. In April 1968 Aberdeen bought a player from Preston North End for a fee of £25,000. Can you name the player in question?

Quiz 4
Questions 61-80

61. In what year and against which club did Willie Miller make his first-team debut for Aberdeen?

62. For what reason did Ally McLeod leave Aberdeen?

63. Who were Aberdeen's opponents in the Scottish Cup final in 1970, and what was the final score?

64. Have Aberdeen ever been knocked out of a European competition on penalties? If so, against which clubs?

65. Willie Miller picked up his first senior medal while playing for which club?

66. On what date (approximately) and against which club did Drew Jarvie score his first hat-trick for the Dons?

67. In what season did Aberdeen first reach the final of the Scottish Cup?

68. Have Aberdeen ever won the Southern Scottish League Cup?

69. In what season did Aberdeen first reach the final of the League Cup?

70. What is the highest defeat Aberdeen have suffered in a League game?

71. When last did Motherwell knock Aberdeen out of the Scottish Cup, up to season 1985/86?

72. In March 1973 Aberdeen bought which player from Hearts?

73. Everton signed a Pittodrie favourite in December 1972. Can you name him?

74. Can you name the official matchday programme for Aberdeen Football Club?

75. Who were the first club to be knocked out of a European competition on penalties?

76. Who were Aberdeen's opponents in the second round of the 1982/83 European Cup Winners Cup?

77. In what year did Eddie Turnbull take over as manager of Aberdeen FC?

78. During 1966 Aberdeen sold which player to Rangers for a fee of £45,000-£50,000?

79. During 1965 Aberdeen bought a player from Morton for a fee of £10,000. During 1967 the same player was involved in a swop deal resulting in this player going to Motherwell and George Murray coming to Pittodrie. Can you name the player in question?

80. During 1966 Aberdeen sold two players to Crystal Palace. Can you name them?

Quiz 5
Questions 81-100

81. In which year was Bobby Clark signed by Aberdeen FC?

82. In 1967 Wolves bought which player from Aberdeen FC?

83. During the European Cup Winners Cup competition, 1983, how many goals did Eric Black score?

84. In what year and month did Alex Ferguson take over as manager of Aberdeen FC?

85. How many goals did Aberdeen score during the European Cup Winners Cup competition in 1983?

86. During the 1983 European Cup Winners Cup competition, how many goals were scored against Aberdeen?

87. Who was the first Aberdeen captain ever to lead two Scottish Cup-winning sides?

88. Has Juventus ever played at Pittodrie? If so, in which month and year?

89. Which team did Aberdeen knock out of the Cup Winners Cup, 1978/79?

90. Has any club ever scored six goals against Aberdeen in a European competition?

91. What was the aggregate score between Aberdeen and Dinamo Tirana in the first round of the European Cup Winners Cup, 1983?

92. Did Aberdeen appear in the 93rd Scottish Cup final?

93. Can you name Aberdeen's manager between 1955 and 1959?

94. Have Aberdeen ever sacked a manager?

95. How many previous managers have Aberdeen had before the arrival of Alex Ferguson?

96. Can you name the author of the book *The Dons*?

97. Can you name the Dons' manager before Ally McLeod but after Eddie Turnbull?

98. Can you name two directors of Aberdeen Football Club, 1986?

99. Where was Neil Simpson born?

100. The Dons signed Jim Leighton from which club?

Quiz 6
Questions 101-120

101. With which English club did John Hewitt have trials?

102. Can you name Aberdeen's first ever manager?

103. Can you name the first ex-Don to win a European Cup Winners medal?

104. In which year did Aberdeen first wear red jerseys?

105. How many years was Dave Halliday manager of Aberdeen Football Club?

106. Aberdeen played their first game at Pittodrie in August 1903. Who were their opponents?

107. In which year did Alex McLeish sign for the Dons?

108. Can you name Aberdeen's manager between 1959 and 1965?

109. During their first season Aberdeen wore what colour of jerseys?

110. Can you name the first Aberdeen player ever to be capped for Scotland?

111. Can you name Aberdeen's longest-serving manager?

112. In what year did Billy McNeill take over as manager of Aberdeen?

113. The Dons signed Alex McLeish from which club?

114. *The Dons* book was written on which anniversary of Aberdeen Football Club?

115. Can you name the Dons' manager between 1924 and 1938?

116. What were Aberdeen's colours between 1904 and 1938?

117. How many League goals did Aberdeen score in the season they were League champions—1979/80?

118. During season 1979/80, three Aberdeen players scored hat-tricks. Can you name them?

119. Dougie Bell previously played for which club prior to the Dons?

120. In season 1979/80 Aberdeen met the same club in the first round of both the League Cup and the Scottish Cup. Can you name the club involved?

Quiz 7
Questions 121-140

121. Prior to being a Dons' player, for which club did Derek McKay play?

122. During mid to late 1960s, Aberdeen transferred Tommy McMillan to which club?

123. Aberdeen signed Dave Robb from which club in 1965?

124. Can you name the Dons' top goalscorer in season 1969/70?

125. In what year was the original Aberdeen Football Club formed?

126. What three Aberdeen teams amalgamated in 1903 to form the present Aberdeen Football Club Ltd.?

127. Since the Premier League started in season 1975/76, can you give Aberdeen's placings up to 1986?

128. In what year were floodlights first introduced to Pittodrie?

129. In what year did fire destroy part of the main stand and offices at Pittodrie?

130. Which Dundee player of the 1950s managed Aberdeen for a short period?

131. Dundee exchanged Gordon Strachan for which Aberdeen player?

132. Can you name the Hungarian internationalist who played for Aberdeen in the early 1970s?

133. Which Aberdeen player scored the fastest goal in Scottish Cup history, up to 1986?

134. Has Alex Ferguson ever played in a Scottish Cup final?

135. Since the Premier League began in 1975/76 until end of season 1985/86 (396 games), can you give approximate amount of League wins Aberdeen have had?

136 In what year did Aberdeen start wearing an all red strip?

137 Who were the first foreign side to win a European tie at Pittodrie?

138. What was the aggregate score in the UEFA Cup 1st round v Ipswich Town, season 1981/82?

139. During 1979 which player scored Aberdeen's 4,000th League goal?

140 Which country did Aberdeen Football Club tour in 1924?

Quiz 8
Questions 141-160

141. In season 1923/24 Aberdeen FC were fined £100 by the SFA. What offence had been committed?

142. In 1910 Aberdeen FC paid out its first benefit to which player?

143. Can you name the player who won a Scottish Cup winners medal with Kilmarnock in 1929 although a signed Aberdeen player?

144. Aberdeen supplied Scotland's very first World Cup goalkeeper in 1954. Can you name him?

145. What was the average wage Aberdeen players received in the early 1930s?

146. Can you name the Aberdeen player who died during the Dons' tour of South Africa in 1937?

147. At the age of 21, which Aberdeen player became the youngest ever captain of a Scottish Cup winning team?

148. Who were the first English team to play at Pittodrie?

149. Did Aberdeen win, lose or draw their first game at Pittodrie on 15 August 1903?

150. Can you name the player who signed for the Dons at the age of 29 and played his last game for the Dons aged 42 in the 1920s? The same player later returned to Pittodrie as a trainer/coach at the age of 53.

151. Can you name the very first player Aberdeen signed after the First World War?

152. Can you name at least three players in the first Aberdeen team to reach the semi-final of a Scottish Cup?

153. The SFA closed Pittodrie for two weeks during season 1911/12. For what reason?

154. During the early 1930s Pittodrie introduced a new creation which was soon to be copied by other clubs throughout the world. What was the creation?

155. Which Aberdeen player of the 1920s and 30s retired from big-time football, having served Aberdeen FC for 21 years?

156. In which year did Archie Glen sign for the Dons?

157. In which year did Archie Glen make his first team debut for Aberdeen?

158. Which country did Aberdeen tour in 1950?

159. In what year did Aberdeen sign Jack Hather, and from which club?

160. From which club did Aberdeen sign Paddy Buckley in the late 1940s, early 1950s?

Quiz 9
Questions 161-180

161. Can you name the Pittodrie cat which had to be destroyed during the early 1950s, on the eve of the Scottish Cup final?

162. What are the pitch dimensions of Pittodrie, 1986?

163. In Division One, season 1962/63, Aberdeen beat which team 10-0 away from home?

164. Can you name Aberdeen's first ever substitute; also in what year was he first called into action?

165. Which Aberdeen player was voted Scottish Sportswriters' Player of the Year in 1979/80?

166. During the 1950s, on how many occasions did Aberdeen appear in a Scottish Cup final?

167. Can you name the scorers of Aberdeen's goals v Lech Poznan in the 2nd Round, 1st leg, European Cup Winners Cup, 1982/83, at Pittodrie?

168. Which team did Alex Ferguson manage before taking over at Pittodrie?

169. Can you name the Aberdeen player who scored an own goal in the 1953/54 Scottish Cup final?

170. Can you name at least five players in the Aberdeen team which played in the Scottish Cup final 1953/54 v Celtic?

171. Which club did Dave Halliday manage directly after quitting as manager of Aberdeen?

172. Which post did Dave Shaw hold at Pittodrie before taking over as manager?

173. Can you name the captain of Aberdeen's League Cup winning team of season 1955/56?

174. Which Aberdeen player of the 1950s retired from football at 28 years of age, to become a fish market porter?

175. Which ex-Aberdeen player won £175,000 on the pools in 1972?

176. Can you give league positions of the Dons from seasons 1954/55 to 1959/60?

177. Can you name at least five players in the Aberdeen team which played in the Scottish Cup final of 1958/59?

178. What was the final score in the Scottish Cup final in 1958/59?

179. What was the financial position of Aberdeen Football Club in 1960?

180. How many Aberdeen players did Eddie Turnbull give free transfers within six weeks of taking over as manager in March 1965?

Quiz 10
Questions 181-200

181. Can you name at least five players in the Aberdeen team which reached the final of the Scottish Cup in season 1966/67?

182. Can you name the Scandinavian player who played for the Dons in the 1960s?

183. What was the adopted name for Aberdeen Football Club during their visit to America in 1967?

184. Can you name the youngest player Aberdeen fielded in the

European Cup Winners competition in 1983?

185. Can you name an Aberdeen player of the 1970s who was banned from playing football in West Germany because of a bribery scandal?

186. What was the capacity of Pittodrie before it became an all-seated stadium?

187. Can you name the Danish player in Aberdeen's Cup-winning side of 1970?

188. Which player won a Scottish Cup winners medal within four months of signing for the Dons at the age of 17 in 1970?

189. Which Aberdeen manager took Zoltan Varga to Pittodrie?

190. What was the duration of Charlie Cooke's service at Pittodrie?

191. Can you name an Aberdeen player of the 1970s who, on being substituted, strode to the touch line, pulled off his shirt and threw it at the manager, and walked out of Pittodrie in disgust, never to play for Aberdeen again?

192. Can you name a Dons' player of the 1950s who got a free transfer from Aberdeen after only one season. This player was later signed by West Ham and played for Scotland in 1959?

193. Which club did Ally McLeod manage before taking over at Pittodrie?

194. Can you name the ex-Aberdeen player who was later signed by Ajax?

195. Can you name the Aberdeen players who were banned from ever appearing in a Scottish national jersey? The ban took place in 1972.

196. Dave Robb was transferred from Aberdeen to which American club?

197. During the late 1960s, which Aberdeen player signed for the now defunct American outfit, Kansas City Spurs?

198. In which country was Neale Cooper born?

199. What was the largest crowd that watched a Dons game during season 1981/82, and what was the occasion?

200. Which Aberdeen manager took Drew Jarvie to Pittodrie?

Picture Quiz 1
Known as Bumper–signed for Aberdeen November 1969–called up to Pittodrie 10 January 1970–now playing for an English side?

Picture Quiz 2
Born in Lanarkshire and signed for the Dons in July 1947 he made his first-team appearance for Aberdeen v Falkirk in February 1950–went on to make 269 appearances for Aberdeen before accepting specialists' advice in 1960 to quit the game?

Quiz 11
Questions 201-220

201. In which year did Drew Jarvie have his Testimonial for the Dons?

202. Including the 1986 Scottish Cup, how many Scottish Cup semi-finals have Aberdeen taken part in?

203. Which player did Aberdeen sign from local side Formartine United in the 1960s?

204. What was the official attendance of the Scottish Cup final 1959, Aberdeen v St. Mirren?

205. Which ex-Aberdeen player later became manager of Kilmarnock?

206. Towards the end of season 1982/83 Motherwell bought which two players from Aberdeen?

207. Aberdeen have met Celtic in the Scottish Cup on 20 occasions, including replays. How many of these encounters have Aberdeen won, up to and including season 1985/86?

208. On 12 February 1983, which Aberdeen player was the first player to score a hat-trick for Aberdeen v Celtic at Parkhead since 1969?

209. Which club did Zoltan Varga play for prior to Aberdeen?

210. At Hampden Park on 24 April, 1937, a new attendance record was set for a Scottish Cup final—146,433. Can you name the two teams taking part?

211. During the late 1940s/1950s, Aberdeen players were the highest paid in Scottish football. What was their weekly wage?

212. Can you name the first Aberdeen player to win the Footballer of the Year award?

213. Which ex-Aberdeen player took over as manager of Alloa in late 1982, thus making him the youngest boss in Scottish football at that time?

214. Can you name the Aberdeen player who was booked on his debut for the first team pool in March 1973?

215. Can you name the Aberdeen player who made his 250th consecutive first team appearance on 23 March 1968 v Motherwell at Fir Park?

216. Can you name the Aberdeen FC Youth Coach in 1983?

217. Can you name at least five players in the Aberdeen team who created a club record for highest amount of goals scored in a Scottish Cup game v Peterhead?

218. Before signing for the Dons, which club did Andy Harrow play for?

219. Can you name the player who formed part of a deal which brought Peter Weir to Pittodrie in 1981?

220. What was the Dons' highest league win during season 1980/81?

Quiz 12
Questions 221-240

221. Which team knocked Aberdeen out of the Scottish Cup in season 1980/81?

222. During season 1980/81, how many goals were scored against Aberdeen in league games only?

223. Name the Belgian goalkeeper signed from a Dutch club who scored on his debut for a Scottish side playing a cup tie in England.

224. During the 1930s Aberdeen had four South Africans on their books. Can you name two of them?

225. In what year did Mark McGhee sign for the Dons?

226. In 1959 Aberdeen signed an Indian ball player who never kicked a ball in earnest for the Dons. Can you name him?

227. During the early 1960s Aberdeen signed a Bermudan player. Can you name him?

228. From what club did Aberdeen sign Mark McGhee?

229. Can you name the Irishman Aberdeen signed in 1974?

230. Can you name two players of the 1960s who joined the Dons from K.B. Copenhagen?

231. Apart from the two players signed from K.B. Copenhagen, can you name another two Scandinavian players who joined the Dons in the 1960s?

232. Can you name the player Aberdeen signed from Washington Whips in 1969?

233. When did John Hewitt make his 200th appearance in the Dons first team? Out of 200 appearances how many were as a substitute?

234. In what year did Joe Harper return to Pittodrie after having spells at Everton and Hibs?

235. Who scored Aberdeen's first goal in a Scottish Cup final?

236. Which Aberdeen player missed a penalty in the 1947 Scottish Cup final?

237. Against which Premier League side did Mark McGhee score his first goal for Aberdeen?

238. Aberdeen have won the Scottish Cup on several occasions. Can you give the original purchase price of the Scottish Cup?

239. How many Aberdeen players in the 1982 cup winning side had previous Scottish Cup medals?

240. In what year did Pittodrie get its first 40,000 plus crowd?

Quiz 13
Questions 241-260

241. During season 1983/84 Aberdeen had a run of 27 games without defeat. Can you name the club that ended that run?

242. Which non-league club did Aberdeen meet in the Scottish Cup 1954, away from home?

243. Can you name the only Aberdonian ever to manage the Dons?

244. Can you name the Polish team Aberdeen beat 9-1 and 8-1 in a tour of Central Europe in 1911?

245. During 1970 Aberdeen met Polish side Gornik Zabrze in a friendly at Pittodrie. What was the final score?

246. What have Alex Ferguson and Stuart Kennedy in common?

247. In July 1981, the Dons travelled to the Faroes to meet Torshavn in a friendly. What was the final score?

248. In what year did Archie Knox become assistant manager at Pittodrie?

249. Before taking up his post as assistant manager at Pittodrie, which club did Archie Knox manage?

250. Previous to Archie Knox, who was assistant manager at Pittodrie?

251. In the Premier League, season 1980/81, how many points divided first and second place?

252. In the League Cup, season 1947/48, Aberdeen beat which team 9-0 in the qualifying section?

253. In the knockout stages of the League Cup, season 1947/48, which team did Aberdeen beat 8-2 at Pittodrie?

254. In the Premier League, season 1982/83, how many points divided third and fourth place?

255. In the Premier League, season 1982/83, how many points divided second and third position?

256. In the Scottish League Division One, season 1967/68, what position did Aberdeen finish up in the League?

257. For which club did Steve Murray play before signing for the Dons in 1970?

258. Can you name Martin Buchan's brother who played for the Dons around the same time?

259. In April 1973 Aberdeen transferred which player to Celtic for a fee of around £50,000?

260. Can you name the player Aberdeen bought from Partick Thistle in 1968 for a fee of around £20,000?

Quiz 14
Questions 261-280

261. In the UEFA Cup, 1981/82, Aberdeen defeated the holders of the trophy. Can you name the beaten side?

262. Can you name the team that knocked Aberdeen out of the UEFA Cup in season 1973/74?

263. In the 1971/72 UEFA Cup, can you name the team that Aberdeen defeated in the first round?

264. During season 1954/55, how many league games did Aberdeen lose?

265. In which season were Aberdeen first runners-up in the League?

266. Can you name the Aberdeen player who was Scotland's leading goal scorer in season 1929/30?

267. In July 1976 which present-day Aberdeen player (1986) had trials with Aston Villa?

268. To the end of season 1985/86, how many goals have Aberdeen scored in European competitions?

269. Up to the end of season 1985/86, how many games have Aberdeen won, lost and drawn in European competitions?

270. Up to the end of season 1985/86, how many English teams have Aberdeen played in European competitions?

271. During season 1982/83, how many league games did Jim Leighton NOT play in?

272. Can you name the Aberdeen player who was voted No. Two under-24 player in Europe by an Italian magazine in 1983?

273. In what position did Aberdeen finish their first season in Scottish League Division One?

274. Can you name the first team Aberdeen played in their first season in Scottish League Division One football?

275. Who were the first team Aberdeen beat in Division One football?

276. In what year did Aberdeen first wear numbers on their jerseys?

277. Up to season 1986, who is the all-time top scorer for Aberdeen?

278. What was Aberdeen's nickname before "The Dons"?

279. In the semi-final of the Scottish Cup in April 1978, which team did Aberdeen beat to get through to the final?

280. During season 1982/83, in how many league games did Aberdeen defeat Rangers?

Picture Quiz 3
Two goal hero for Aberdeen FC in their Scottish Cup success of 1970?

Quiz 15
Questions 281-300

281. In season 1980/81 Scottish Cup, how many games did Aberdeen play at Pittodrie?

282. Can you name the teams Aberdeen knocked out of the Scottish Cup, 1982/83?

283. What stage did Aberdeen reach in the Scottish Cup in season 1977/78?

284. Can you name the Dons players that were included in the 1978 Scotland World Cup squad?

285. In what year was Billy McNeill voted Manager of the Year?

286. In which year did Walker McCall first sign for the Dons?

287. In January, 1932, Sunderland paid £2,000 for which Aberdeen player?

288. Prior to Joe Harper, who was the Dons top goal scorer?

289. Can you name a typical Dons line-up of 1959?

290. Can you name the Dons top goal scorer of 1957/58?

291. Which team knocked Aberdeen out of the 1965 Scottish Cup?

292. During season 1969/70, which Aberdeen goalkeeper played several games in the first team as an outfield player?

293. In what year was there a takeover bid made for control of Aberdeen FC?

294. Who skippered the Dons during season 1958/59?

295. Can you name the player Aberdeen signed as an outfield player, but who, within a few years, was Scotland's World Cup keeper?

296. In which year did Aberdeen have its first ever 20,000 plus crowd?

297. Can you name an Aberdeen player of mid/late 1950s who was born in Kintore (Aberdeenshire)?

298. Can you name the first Aberdeen player to score a hat-trick for the Dons in a European competition?

299. Apart from Bobby Clark and Jim Leighton, can you name another two keepers who have kept goal for Aberdeen in a

European competition?

300. Against which team did Jim Leighton first keep goal for Aberdeen in a European competition?

Quiz 16
Questions 301-320

301. How many first team appearances (approximately) did Arthur Graham make while a Dons player?

302. Can you name Aberdeen's manager when they first won the Scottish Cup?

303. Can you name Aberdeen's reserve keeper in the later stages of season 1967/68.

304. Which Aberdeen player was given a free transfer in lieu of a benefit at the end of season 1976/77?

305. Which Aberdeen player scored Scotland's goal v Wales at Hampden in May 1980?

306. Can you name Aberdeen's youngest signed full-time player in 1980?

307. Can you name Aberdeen's best-known talent spotter of all time?

308. Which Aberdeen player(s) were included in Scotland's pool to meet Ireland at Hampden in March 1981?

309. Can you name the first team to beat Aberdeen in a league game in season 1984/85?

310. Aberdeen played a Testimonial game v Manchester United in August 1983—for which former Aberdeen player?

311. During season 1979/80, what was Aberdeen's highest win in the Premier League?

312. On how many occasions did Aberdeen defeat Rangers in the Premier League in season 1979/80?

313. Which Aberdeen player was in the Scottish team which was defeated 7-2 by England in April 1955?

314. Which club did Billy McNeill manage before taking over at Pittodrie?

315. In what year did Aberdeen first meet Rangers in a final of the Scottish Cup?

316. Ipswich Town played at Pittodrie on Saturday, 7 August, 1982. What was the occasion?

317. While an Aberdeen player, on how many occasions was Drew Jarvie sent off?

318. In 1967, which player did Aberdeen buy from Leeds United for approximately £12,500?

319. In the League Cup, season 1972/73, Aberdeen beat which team 8-0 in the first leg, but lost the second leg 3-2?

320. What was the lowest attendance for a league game at Pittodrie in season 1981/82?

Quiz 17
Questions 321-340

321. During season 1981/82, how many league games did Jim Leighton NOT play in for the Dons?

322. Who were the Dons opponents in Willie Miller's Testimonial match on 16 August 1981?

323. How many League appearances did Drew Jarvie make for Aberdeen?

324. Can you name the first Aberdeen player to win a Scottish Cup badge?

325. Up to season 1985/86, when was the last time Aberdeen met St. Mirren in a cup final?

326. Between 8 February and 19 April 1947, how many consecutive cup ties did Aberdeen play in?

327. In which year did Aberdeen make their 21st Scottish Cup semi-final appearance?

328. While manager of St. Mirren, Alex Ferguson signed which player and in 1983 took that same player to Pittodrie?

329. Can you name an Aberdeen player of the late 50s, early 60s, who started his career with Raith Rovers, then signed for Aberdeen, then St. Mirren where he was later to become manager?

330. Can you name the first Rumanian side ever to play at Pittodrie?

331. Which English team played at Pittodrie in Jack Hutton's benefit in 1924?

332. Aberdeen reached the final of which cup in August 1951?

333. Who scored Aberdeen's first Premier League goal in season 1983/84?

334. How many goals did Eric Black score v Raith Rovers at Pittodrie in the League Cup, second round, first leg, on 24 August 1983?

335. How many league appearances did Willie Mills make for the Dons in the 1930s?

336. Which is Aberdeen's record defeat in a first class game?

337. Which Aberdeen player, at the age of 33, made his International debut for Scotland in 1911?

338. By what nickname was the Dons star of the 30s, George Hamilton, known as?

339. Can you name the first Dons player to play in a World Cup?

340. Who were Aberdeen's opponents in the first round of the Drybrough Cup in August, 1980?

Quiz 18
Questions 341-360

341. Against which club did Billy Stark score his first hat-trick for the Dons?

342. Against which club did Ian Porteous score his first competition first-team goal for the Dons?

343. What was Aberdeen's highest cup win in the Scottish Cup in season 1979/80?

344. In season 1939/40, how many league games did Aberdeen play?

345. What team did Aberdeen play in a challenge match at Pittodrie on 12 August, 1980?

346. Against which club did Billy Stark make his Aberdeen debut in a Premier game?

347. How many Scottish caps did Dons star of the 30s, Willie Mills, have?

348. Who scored Aberdeen's first goal in a Hampden Cup final?

349. Against which club did Aberdeen play their last game in the old First Division?

350. Which Aberdeen player was picked for Scotland v Wales at Cardiff in 1935?

351. Can you name the former Aberdeen skipper who was in the Elgin City team that met the Dons in a Scottish Cup game in January 1971?

352. Can you name the only Aberdeen player to get a Scottish cap between 1958 and 1966?

353. While a Dons player, how many appearances did Graham Leggat make for Scotland?

354. How many Aberdeen keepers since 1950 up to 1986 have played for Scotland (excluding Youth Internationalists, Under 21s etc)?

355. How many full Scottish Caps has Joe Harper?

356. Up to September 1986, what is the highest win the Dons have recorded since Alex Ferguson became manager of Dons?

357. How many hat-tricks did Eric Black score during season 1982/83?

358. What was Aberdeen's highest defeat in the League Cup in season 1982/83?

359. Approximately what was the total attendance at all League Cup games at Pittodrie in season 1982/83?

360. Which team knocked Aberdeen out of the League Cup in season 1982/83?

Quiz 19
Questions 361-380

361. Did Aberdeen win, lose or draw the first Premier home game in season 1982/83?

362 How many goals did Aberdeen have scored against them in the League Cup, season 1982/83?

Picture Quiz 4
This man was manager of Aberdeen FC from 1955 to 1959—and was known as "Faither"
by his players?

Picture Quiz 5
Signed from Morton in October 1969—later to become known as the "King"?

363. Which Aberdeen player scored a hat-trick v Dundee in the League Cup, season 1982/83?

364. How many goals did Mark McGhee score during the European Cup Winners competition 1982/83?

365. Who was Aberdeen's top goal scorer in the League Cup competition, 1982/83?

366. Who scored Aberdeen's goal in the European Cup Winners Cup competition, 1982/83, v Lech Poznan, second leg?

367. Can you name the only team to beat Aberdeen in the European Cup Winners Cup competition, season 1982/83?

368. Between season 1967/68 and season 1980/81 (both seasons included), how many games did Aberdeen play in European competition)?

369. Which player did Falconer substitute in European Cup Winners Cup competition semi-final, second leg, v Waterschie, 1982-83?

370. How many Dons players scored goals in the European Cup Winners Cup competition, 1982/83?

371. During the European Cup Winners Cup competition, season 1982/83, can you name three Aberdeen players who were substituted after scoring a goal?

372. Over 3,000 punters attended Pittodrie to see which Aberdeen player make his return to competitive football v St. Johnstone reserves in which the young Dons won 10-2, in March 1981?

373. From which club did Aberdeen buy Bobby Clark?

374. In what season did Celtic beat Aberdeen 7-1 at Parkhead?

375. On leaving Aberdeen, Dave Smith joined which club?

376. Aberdeen sold Tommy Craig to which English club?

377. Bobby Clark got his first senior honour at Hampden Park in 1967 in which Scotland won 3-2. Who were Scotland's opponents?

378. During 1970/71, Bobby Clark kept a clean sheet for how many successive games?

379. Who were the Dons opponents in the Scottish Cup semi-final, season 1958-59?

380. In the League Cup, season 1977/78, Aberdeen defeated a team 7-1. In the same season the Dons defeated the same team 2-0 in the Scottish Cup. Can you name the team in question?

Quiz 20
Questions 381-400

381. Meadowbank Thistle made their first ever visit to Pittodrie in a League Cup game in September 1977. What was the score?

382. Between 1961 and 1969 how many first team appearances did Ally Shewan make for the Dons?

383. Which team did Aberdeen meet in the semi-final of the 1969-70 Scottish Cup?

384. Where was the venue of the semi-final of the 1969/70 Scottish Cup?

385. Which team did Aberdeen beat in the first round of the Scottish Cup, season 1969/70?

386. What is the full name of the Icelandic team who were Aberdeen's opponents in their first appearance in a European competition?

387. Who skippered Aberdeen in the 1967 Scottish Cup final?

388. Which leading Dutch side played a friendly at Pittodrie in August 1973?

389. Where was the venue of the League Cup semi-final, Aberdeen v Hibs, season 1978/79?

390. Which Dutch club played at Pittodrie in April 1972?

391. In April 1971, Aberdeen played Eintracht at Pittodrie. What was the final score?

392. Aberdeen met Chelsea at Pittodrie in 1955 and 1967. Can you give the score on both occasions?

393. In December 1970 which Aberdeen player signed for Kilmarnock?

394. Which player did Aberdeen sign from Chelsea in 1970?

395. In 1974 which player did Aberdeen sign from Dundee United?

396. For which club did Martin Buchan play before being called up by the Dons in 1964?

397. Before becoming a Dons player in 1965, which club did Ernie McGarr play for?

398. Before becoming a Dons player in 1965, which club did Jim Hermiston play for?

399. What is the name of the fictional character associated with the Dons?

400. In which year did John McMaster sign for the Dons?

Quiz 21
Questions 401-420

401. In season 1970/71 how many league goals were scored against the Dons in their first 11 home games?

402. What was the score when Aberdeen met Elgin City in a Scottish Cup match in January 1971?

403. Between 1931 and 1971, Morton played 21 games at Pittodrie. Of the 21 games, how many did Morton win?

404. In which year did Joe Harper first sign for the Dons?

405. In 1969 Aberdeen signed two players from Rangers. Can you name them?

406. What was Aberdeen's highest win in season 1973/74?

407. Who scored Aberdeen's goals in the first round, first leg of the European Cup Winners Cup, 1983/84, v Akranes?

408. How many teams were Aberdeen defeated by in the League, season 1935/36?

409. How many League points did Aberdeen finish with in season 1935/36?

410. What stage did the Dons reach in the Presidents Cup?

411. In what year did Aberdeen compete in the Presidents Cup?

412. Whose goal clinched Aberdeen's first ever League championship?

413. Against which club did Aberdeen clinch their first ever League championship?

414. Can you name at least five players in the Aberdeen team who, in a League game, suffered Aberdeen's record defeat v Celtic in January 1965 at Parkhead?

415. Up to the end of season 1982/83, what was the highest Aberdeen had paid for a player?

416. Up to season 1983/84, can you name Aberdeen's highest-priced transfer export?

417. Which team did Aberdeen play in the Anglo-Scottish Cup at Pittodrie on 1 October 1975?

418. What was the duration of Jack Hather's stay at Pittodrie?

419. When did Jack Hather make his first team debut for the Dons?

420. In what year did Billy Little sign for the Dons?

Quiz 22
Questions 421-440

421. In which year did Ian Hare become a Dons player?

422. Who were Aberdeen's opponents in their first competitive European game since winning the 1982/83 European Cup Winners Cup?

423. How many League goals did Aberdeen score during season 1935/36?

424. What is Aberdeen's highest League Cup defeat?

425. Up to the end of season 1985/86, Aberdeen have lost three League Cup finals since the Second World War. Can you give season, score and opponents?

426. Which team in season 1962/63 knocked Aberdeen out of the Scottish Cup, and in the same season were relegated, having only two victories out of 34 League games?

427. Aberdeen gave which Scottish club their record defeat?

428. What is Aberdeen's record League Cup win?

429. Who scored Aberdeen's goals v S.V. Hamburg in the UEFA Cup, third round, at Pittodrie in November 1981?

430. In the League Cup, 1970/71, Aberdeen beat which team 7-3 at Pittodrie?

431. During the European Cup Winners Cup, season 1982/83, which tie involving Aberdeen attracted the largest crowd?

432. Approximately how many people attended Aberdeen's home games in the European Cup Winners competition, 1982/83? (Answer to nearest 3,000).

433. Aberdeen played 31 consecutive League games without defeat. Can you name the team that ended that run in December 1980?

434. In December 1980 Aberdeen put in a written offer of £160,000 (which was rejected) for which player?

435. What was Aberdeen's highest League win in season 1980/81?

436. Can you name the player who made most first team appearances for the Dons in season 1980/81?

437. Can you name the Aberdeen player who, on his first team debut, scored a goal within two minutes in a League Cup match in season 1951/52?

438. In which season did Clydebank register their first win over Aberdeen in a League game?

439. In a tournament held at Pittodrie in August 1981, can you name the three English clubs taking part?

440. Aberdeen just missed relegation in season 1975/76. Can you name the team that were eventually relegated?

Quiz 23
Questions 441-460

441. Can you name the Aberdeen player who received the "Golden Ball" Award in November 1980?

442. Can you name the Aberdeen goalkeeper of the 20s who played an entire Scottish Cup game wearing a waterproof coat?

443. Which Aberdeen player signed from Montrose scored 38 league goals for the Dons in season 1929/30?

Picture Quiz 6
Perhaps Aberdeen's most flamboyant manager ever, who had everyone believing that Scotland could win the World Cup?

444. Can you name the Aberdeen team that won the Drybrough Cup in August 1980?

445. In the Scottish Cup, season 1966/67, Aberdeen defeated two teams 5-0. Can you name the teams in question?

446. In which European competition did Aberdeen take part, season 1977/78?

447. In which European competition did Aberdeen take part, season 1970/71?

448. Against which club did Brian Mitchell make his European debut for the Dons?

449. Between seasons 1967/68 and 1981/82, only one team failed to make the final of a European competition after accounting for the Dons. Can you name the team in question?

450. Who were Aberdeen's opponents at the official opening of Pittodrie Park?

451. In which year was a cover first erected over the Beach End at Pittodrie?

452. In which year did the bench-type seating disappear from the South Stand at Pittodrie?

453. How many European games did Martin Buchan play in while a Dons player?

454. Approximately how many first team appearances did Martin Buchan make while a Dons player?

455. Which Highland League side was John McMaster farmed out to in his early days as a signed Aberdeen player?

456. Which Aberdeen junior club did Doug Rougvie play for before being called up to senior grade by Aberdeen?

457. Which stage of the Scottish Cup did Aberdeen reach in season 1977/78?

458. Against which country did Martin Buchan make his first full appearance for Scotland?

459. Who were Aberdeen's opponents in the first round of the European Cup Winners Cup in season 1978/79?

460. Who were Aberdeen's opponents in the first round of the UEFA Cup in season 1973/74?

Quiz 24
Questions 461-480

461. Can you name the club that knocked Aberdeen out of the League Cup in season 1983/84?

462. How many league goals did Doug Rougvie score in LEAGUE CUP games in season 1982/83?

463. Who scored Aberdeen's goal(s) in the semi-final of the Scottish Cup in season 1982/83?

464. Apart from a European Cup Winners game, what other important event happened at Pittodrie on 3 November 1983?

465. Who were the first team to score a goal against Aberdeen in the League Cup in season 1983/84?

466. Against which country did Doug Rougvie get his first full cap?

467. Against which club did Tommy McIntyre make his first team debut for the Dons (1983)?

468. Against which club did Willie Miller make his 600th appearance for the Dons?

469. Against which club did Stewart McKimmie make his first team debut for the Dons (1983)?

470. From which club did the Dons sign Stewart McKimmie?

471. In which European competition did Stewart McKimmie make his debut for the Dons?

472. Who scored Aberdeen's goal(s) in the European Super Cup final, second leg, at Pittodrie?

473. A former Newcastle United player played in goal for the Dons in the early 1960s. Can you name him?

474. Dundee United signed two Dons players in the mid-1950s, during their Second Division days. Can you name them?

475. Who were the first Aberdeen players to win Under-23 honours?

476. Can you name an Aberdeen player who became a minister in Liverpool in the late 1920s?

477. What was Aberdeen's biggest League win in season 1970/71?

478. Who was Aberdeen's Scottish International goalkeeper contemporary with Bobby Clark?

479. In 1969 two Aberdeen players were transferred to England, each for a fee of around £100,000. Who were they?

480. In what year did Aberdeen meet Deveronvale in a Scottish Cup tie, and what was the score?

Quiz 25
Questions 481-500

481. When last did a game have to be abandoned at Pittodrie due to weather conditions, previous to Dons v St. Johnstone 3 January 1984?

482. Can you name the Aberdeen player who was voted "Player of the Year" in season 1973/74, by the Scottish Professional Footballers Association?

483. In a replay in the 1962 Scottish Cup v Clyde, what was the final score?

484. How many goals did Norman Davidson score in the replay of the Scottish Cup v Brechin City at Brechin in 1960?

485. Against which club did Billy Little make his first team debut for the Dons in the 1950s?

486. Where was Duncan Davidson born? (Player 1970s/80s).

487. Aberdeen beat Airdrie 6-2 away from home on 12 October 1957. How many goals did Graham Leggat score?

488. Aberdeen beat which team 10-0 at Pittodrie on 13 October 1962?

489. Name the Welshman who joined the Dons from Swindon Town in 1948?

490. Can you name the player Aberdeen signed from Leicester City in November 1971?

491. Can you name the former Don who later joined Rapid Vienna?

492. How many League goals did George Hamilton score for the Dons in season 1946/47?

493. Can you name a former Aberdeen player of the 1950s that became head coach for Toronto Metros in 1971?

494. In 1969, Aberdeen signed which player from Rangers?

495. Between season 1931/32 and season 1970/71, how many games did Morton win at Pittodrie—(League, League Cup, Scottish Cup and friendlies included)?

496. In which year did the Dons sign Jim Hermiston?

497. Against which club did Harry Melrose first skipper the Dons (1966)?

498. In which year did the Dons first meet Falkirk in a Scottish Cup match?

499. Can you name the Dons leading goal scorer in season 1963/64?

500. From which club did Aberdeen sign Jim Hermiston?

Crossword 1

Quiz 26
Crossword 1

Clues Down

2. A certain Mr McLeod, one-time Dons' manager? (4)

3. Without a doubt Scotland's No. 1 keeper? (8)

4/8 Beaten by Aberdeen on 11 May 1983? (4, 6)

5. Present-day captain? (6)

8. See 4 down.

9. Aberdeen's opponents when they first won the Scottish Cup? (4)

10. Pittodrie's favourite one had to be destroyed on eve of Scottish Cup final 1953/54? (3)

13. The nickname given to a Dons' favourite of the 1970s? (6)

15. The home of Aberdeen Football Club? (9)

19. This end of Pittodrie is reserved for visiting support? (5)

20. Big Doug fae Fife? (7)

24. It's the ref's duty to impose this on the field of play? (3)

26. Beating Real Madrid may have been looked upon by some as this type of result? (5)

27. Short for Aberdeen Football Club? (1,1,1)

29. At most other grounds the supporters have to stand, but at Pittodrie supporters can do this. (3)

Clues Across

1. Without one there would be no game. (4)

4. The boss on the field. (3)

5. Doug Rougvie drinks a lot of this. (4)

6. - - - together. (3)

7. Name of the Pittodrie tea lady perhaps? (3)

8. Has the same Christian name as the Dons' manager. (7)

11. The females all thought Black and Hewitt were this. (3)

12. The Dons' keeper of the 1950s/1960s was often referred to by this name. (3)

14. The Dons are always there or thereabout. (3)

16. A certain Mr Sullivan who joined Celtic from the Dons? (3)

17. - - - Robertson, a Don in the making? (3)

18. Perhaps some day it will be held at Pittodrie. (3)

21. The Dons almost had a top twenty - - - with European song. (3)

22. Peter - - - - (4)

23. This Doug has a surname with a ring to it? (4)

25. This Rangers from Aberdeen—could well be in the Highland League by now? (4)

28. Mr - - - - - - - - - of course? (8)

30. Aberdeen scored this amount of goals in a Scottish Cup replay v Clyde. (2)

31. This Sabastian has no connection with Aberdeen? (3)

32. Aberdeen's best known Super Sub? (6)

33. By using his head this Aberdeen player can make it this type of day for the opposition? (5)

Picture Quiz 7
Signed from local junior side Formartine United in 1960–had an unbroken run of 314
first-team games for Aberdeen FC starting from October 1963 to May 1969?

Crossword 2

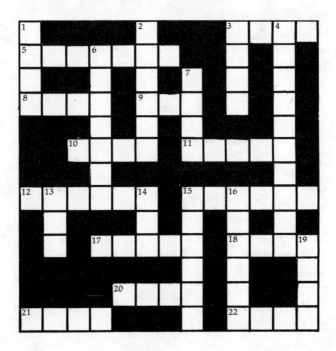

Quiz 27
Crossword 2

Clues Down

1. Dons' Swiss opponents in European Cup Winners Cup, 1982/83? (4)

2. The Bayern game provided plenty of this at Pittodrie? (6)

3. Their home is at Easter Road? (4)

4. Bobby Watson quit as their manager at end of season 1983/84. (10)

6. For some, this would not be the same without watching a football game. (7).

7. Many a player has been thrown in at this end. (4)

13. Short for United? (3)

14. You don't see much of them at football matches? (3)

15/16 This German outfit provided the opposition for perhaps the best game ever seen at Pittodrie. (6, 6)

19. This type of Street is home for St. Mirren. (4)

Clues Across

3. Pittodrie is this for the Dons. (4)

5. UEFA Cup holders that the Dons sent packing in the first round in 1981/82. (7)

8. The Dons scored this amount of goals against Raith Rovers at Pittodrie in the League Cup, first leg. (4)

9. The type of land where Akranes come from. (3)

10. Aberdeen have a number of players still in this age group. (4)

11/20A Dons' favourite. (5, 4)

12. A shock result in the Scottish Cup can mean this type of exit for a Premier team. (6)

15. This type of footwear gave an ex-Don his nickname. (6)

17. This Mr Yorston, a Dons star of yesteryear, had the same Christian name as a Crossroads star. (5)

18. If your football coupon is this it loses it's worth. (4)

20. See 11 Across. (4)

21. Short for Aberdeen. (4)

22. Given their full title, they are known as Brighton and - - - - Albion. (4)

Quiz 28

Jumbled up are the names of ten players who have played for Aberdeen in the past ten years. Some have now left Pittodrie; others have retired from football altogether; some are still turning out for the Dons. Who are they?

1. G G R E I O O U D V U
2. L N I O S D V U A M L
3. R A Y D H W O N A R
4. B R C I K L A E C
5. A J R E H R P O E
6. E E D A V J W R R I
7. O C D D I N A V S N D U N A
8. Y K B B B A C O R L
9. L L L L I I I R E E W M
10. B E S V C A L I T E B R H A

Quiz 29

Hidden amongst the letters below are the names of 21 Dons' players past and present. Can you name them?

```
Q G K S B E L L M Q B C S L
L O R V K U U Q U R O L Z A
S B L A C K C U N G E A M B
L R Q P H J O H R U L R V Z
S T S T R A C H A N E K U N
W E I R W R M N O N C D O W
S X M V U V I R O B B T U H
M B P M O I L C E N S K T A
I A S Z P E L E I G H T O N
T H O G G A E F O G H L R R
H Y N H F G R O U G V I E O
L E F I D S H E W A N O P W
G D A V I D S O N J K Q S R
```

Quiz 30
Questions 501-520

501. In what season did a team last win the Scottish Cup three times in a row, prior to the Dons achieving this in season 1983/84?

502. How many first team appearances did Fred Martin make with the Dons?

503. Can you name the first club to beat the Dons in a European competition at Pittodrie since Liverpool beat them in 1980?

504. How many goals did Gordon Strachan score in League Cup games in season 1983/84?

505. Which former Aberdeen player had his autobiography published towards the end of season 1983/84?

506. In which European competition did Aberdeen compete in season 1983/84?

507. What were the scores in both legs of Aberdeen v Juventus UEFA cup games in 1971?

508. In what year did Aberdeen first meet Celtic in a Scottish Cup semi-final?

509. Jock Buchanan (Rangers) became the first player to be sent off in a Scottish Cup final in 1929. Which Aberdeen player became only the second player to be sent off in a major Scottish final?

510. Which Aberdeen player was voted Scottish Football Writers' Player of the Year in season 1983/84?

511. In season 1967/68 Aberdeen FC were the first British club to introduce an American idea into British football—what was this innovation?

512. Against which club did Gordon Strachan make his last Premier League appearance for the Dons?

513. Can you name the Dons' top scorer in Premier League games in 1983/84?

514. What was the for and against goal tally for the Dons in Premier League games in season 83/84?

515. How many goals did Peter Weir score during the Dons Scottish Cup run in season 1983/84?

516. How many Premier League points did Aberdeen have in the season they won the Premier Championship 1979/80?

517. During season 1983/84, Willie Miller was the Dons recognised skipper, but who skippered the Dons in their last Premier League game in season 1983/84?

518. Out of 36 Premier League games played by the Dons in season 1983/84, on how many occasions did they deny their opponents a goal?

519. What was the average home gate for Premier games played at Pittodrie in season 1983/84?

520. Against which club did Aberdeen draw their first Premier League game at Pittodrie in season 1983/84? Also, in which month?

Quiz 31
Questions 521-540

521. Can you name the Aberdeen player who was awarded the Mr Superfit award and Man of the Match in the Scottish Cup quarter-final v Dundee at Dens Park in March 1986?

522. Can you name the first Aberdeen player to be booked in season 1983/84?

523. Against which club did Stewart McKimmie score his first Premier League goal for the Dons?

524. Who scored the winning goal for Aberdeen in the Scottish Cup final in 1983/84?

525. What was the score after 90 minutes in the Scottish Cup final 1983/84?

526. Can you name the team Aberdeen knocked out of the semi-final of the Scottish Cup, season 1983/84?

527. Can you name the venue of the Scottish Cup semi-final which involved Aberdeen, season 1983/84?

528. Can you name the only Aberdeen player to be sent off in season 1983/84?

529. Can you name the only other team apart from Aberdeen that has won the Scottish Cup three times in a row this century?

530. Against which club did Paul Wright make his first team debut for the Dons? Also, what was his age?

531. How many Aberdeen players were booked at Tannadice in the Scottish Cup quarter-final, season 1983/84? Also, name the players in question.

532. Who was Aberdeen's top goal scorer in European Cup games, season 1985/86?

533. Against which club did Doug Rougvie score two goals in a Premier League game, season 1983/84?

534. Aberdeen set up a new Premier League points record in season 1983/84. How many points did they have?

535. How many Premier League goals did Gordon Strachan score from the penalty spot in season 1983/84?

536. Can you name the teams which defeated Aberdeen in the Premier League at Pittodrie, season 1983/84?

537. Can you give the approximate amount of spectators who attended the Dons eighteen home Premier games, season 1983/84?

538. How many League games did Aberdeen play between 22 October 1983 and 3 March 1984 without a defeat?

539. Can you name the Aberdeen player who was signed by SV Hamburg at the end of season 1983/84 for a fee in the region of £280,000?

540. What were the receipts from Aberdeen's very first game at Pittodrie?

Quiz 32
Questions 541-560

541. Can you name the Dons players who were in the Scotland side in the World Cup of 1954?

542. In Scottish Cup games 1983/84, Aberdeen had four players who were booked on two occasions. Can you name them?

543. Can you name the teams that were in the same section as the Dons in the League Cup, season 1983/84?

544. At the end of season 1983/84, can you name the clubs that were battling for the services of Gordon Strachan?

545. Against which club did Gordon Strachan make his last appearance for the Dons at Pittodrie?

546. Which Aberdeen player scored a hat-trick in the European Cup Winners Cup quarter-final, 2nd leg, at Pittodrie v Ujpest Dozsa, season 1983/84?

547. Who scored Aberdeen's 100th goal in a European competition, and against which club?

548. What unusual incident happened in a match at Pittodrie, Aberdeen v Dundee, on 31 December 1983?

549. Who scored Aberdeen's first Premier League goal of season 1983/84?

550. On how many occasions did opposing teams score own goals when playing against Aberdeen in season 1983/84? (Premier games only).

551. Can you name the two Dons players who were in the Scotland squad in the 1978 World Cup?

552. Did Aberdeen have any players in the 1974 Scotland World Cup squad?

553. Can you name two Dons players of season 1983/84 who scored the goals in a Scottish Cup match, but never scored in any Premier League game?

554. During season 1983/84, which Aberdeen player was booked most often in all first-class games?

555. During the Scottish Cup, 1983/84, which one of the following players did not score a goal for the Dons in the competition?

Eric Black, John Hewitt, Ian Porteous, Ian Angus?

556. Can you name all the goal scorers for the Dons in European Cup Winners Cup competition, Season 1983/84?

557. How many penalty saves did Jim Leighton make in the Premier League games, season 1983/84?

558. Against which club did Aberdeen clinch the League Championship title in season 1983/84?

559. Can you name the club which ended Aberdeen's run of sixteen league games without defeat in season 1983/84?

560. Who were Aberdeen's opponents in the semi-final of the League Cup in season 1983/84?

Quiz 33
Questions 561-580

561. Can you name the only Aberdeen player included in Scotland's World Cup squad of 1958?

562. How many Premier League goals did the following Dons players score in season 1983/84: (1) Stewart McKimmie; (2) Alex McLeish; (3) Peter Weir?

563. In the Premier League, season 1983/84, two Aberdeen players missed from the penalty spot. Can you name them?

564. Apart from Gordon Strachan, only two other Dons players scored from the penalty spot in season 1983/84. Can you name them?

565. Against which club did Ian Robertson make his first team debut for the Dons?

566. Against which club did Eric Black miss from the spot in the League Cup, season 1983/84?

567. Can you name the teams that defeated Aberdeen in the Premier League, season 1983/84?

568. Can you name the only team to score three goals against the Dons in a Premier League game in season 1983/84?

569. In the Premier League, season 1983/84, Aberdeen scored five goals against four teams—can you name the teams in question?

570. Who scored Aberdeen's goal in the Scottish Cup quarter-final replay, season 1983/84?

571. Can you name the Aberdeen players who were in Scotland's World Cup squad in 1982?

572. How many Scottish caps did Graham Leggat get in his full career?

573. On leaving the Dons, which clubs did Billy Wishart sign for?

574. Chelsea signed which player from the Dons at the end of season 1983/84?

575. Which former Dons player signed for Oldham Athletic at the age of 35 at the beginning of season 1984/85?

576. Which country did the Dons tour pre-season 1984/85?

577. Against which club did Tommy McQueen make his first team debut for the Dons in a competitive match?

578. Can you name the first Aberdeen player to score a goal in the Premier League, season 1984/85?

579. Can you name the player the Dons signed from Stirling Albion mid-1985?

580. At the start of season 1984/85 the Dons tried but were unsuccessful in getting which Dons' favourite of the 1970s on a two-month loan from Manchester United?

Quiz 34
Questions 581-600

581. Against which club did Aberdeen play their very first Scottish Cup tie at Pittodrie?

582. Against which club did Frank McDougall make his Premier League debut for the Dons?

583. Which appointment did Dons manager, Alex Ferguson, accept mid-August 1984?

584. In which competition did Brian Grant make his first team debut for the Dons?

Picture Quiz 8
In which season did this Aberdeen line up win the Scottish Cup?

Picture Quiz 9
Manager of Aberdeen FC–the first time they won the Scottish Cup?

585. Can you name the only Aberdonian in the Dons' Scottish Cup winning side of 1947?

586. When Aberdeen Football Club were first formed, how many shares were there, and what was the cost per share?

587. Can you give the exact date Aberdeen Football Club came into being?

588. Can you name the former Aberdeen assistant manager whose Division Two side, Cowdenbeath, knocked Premier side St. Mirren out of the Skol Cup, season 1984/85?

589. Can you name the very first trainer of Aberdeen Football Club?

590. Can you name Aberdeen's very first skipper?

591. Can you name the very first player ever to score a goal for the Dons?

592. Which player scored Aberdeen's 600th Premier League goal?

593. Against which club and in which year did Jim Leighton play his first Premier League game for the Dons?

594. Has John Hewitt ever scored a hat trick v Celtic or Rangers?

595. Can you name Aberdeen's top goal scorer in their very first season?

596. Who was assistant manager at Pittodrie when Billy McNeill was manager?

597. Can you name at least five Aberdeen players who were in the team for their very first game in 1903?

598. Did Aberdeen win, lose or draw their very first Scottish Cup game; also who were their opponents?

599. Which cup did Aberdeen win in their very first season 1903/04?

600. Can you name the famous Celtic outside right who later played for Aberdeen?

Quiz 35
Questions 601-620

601. Can you name the Aberdeen player who first skippered the Dons in a League game v Stirling Albion away from home on 17 December 1966?

Picture Quiz 10
This man was responsible for bringing a galaxy of stars to Aberdeen FC over the years?

602. Can you name the three Dons players in the Scotland Under-23 team who played v England Under-23s at Pittodrie on 18 December 1974?

603. Can you name the player Aberdeen signed from Queen's Park in 1965 who made his debut for the Dons in a Summer Cup tie against Dundee in the same year?

604. What was Aberdeen's highest League win in season 1985/86?

605. Can you name the Aberdeen player involved in an exchange deal in September 1971 which brought Bertie Miller to Pittodrie?

606. Can you name the player Aberdeen signed from Banks O'Dee in May 1954, who was later transferred to Chelsea in 1956? Two years later he moved to Leicester City, but ended his playing career with Bath City.

607. Can you name the player Aberdeen signed from Banks O'Dee in 1965?

608. In which year was Dons manager, Alex Ferguson, transferred from Rangers to Falkirk, and what was the fee involved?

609. Can you name at least four clubs Dons manager Alex Ferguson has played for?

610. Can you name the Dons player of the 1930s who, on being on the Dons books for 15 years, left Aberdeen to become player/coach of Elgin City?

611. Against which club did Neil Simpson make his 200th senior appearance for the Dons (1984)?

612. Can you name the first Scottish player to be transferred from a Scottish club to an English club for a fee of £100,000?

613. Can you name the Aberdeen player(s) who misssed from the penalty spot in the shoot-out, European Cup, 1st round v Dynamo Berlin, season 1984/85?

614. In the European Cup, season 1984/85, can you name the scorer of Aberdeen's goal in the second leg v Dynamo Berlin?

615. Can you name the non-League side who knocked Aberdeen out of the Scottish Cup, season 1906/07?

616. Can you name the Irish internationalist Aberdeen bought from Middlesbrough in season 1906/07?

617. Can you name the former Aberdeen goalkeeper who made his football comeback at the age of 39 for Forres mechanics in the Highland League Cup final, season 1984/85?

618. Can you name the only club who are still in existence, and who have played in the same league as Aberdeen but have yet to beat Aberdeen in a League game?

619. Between season 1904 and the end of season 1985/86, in all League matches, can you name the team that Aberdeen have scored most against?

620. In all League games played by Aberdeen 1903/04 to the end of season 1985/86, only five teams have scored more goals against Aberdeen than Aberdeen have scored against them. Can you name the five teams in question?

Quiz 36
Questions 621-640

621. Can you name the Dons top goal scorer in season 1958/59?

622. In the second leg of the Super Cup 1983/84 played at Pittodrie, how many corner kicks were awarded to each team?

623. Can you name the former Aberdeen player who was sentenced to five months in prison for a football bribes charge in 1965?

624. An unusual substitution took place in a Rangers v Aberdeen League match played at Ibrox on Wednesday, 3 September 1969. What was unusual about the substitution?

625. Can you give an approximate date the Dons shop opened, and where was it situated?

626. Can you name the player Aberdeen signed from East Stirling in 1961?

627. Can you name the Aberdeen player transferred to Stoke in 1963?

628. In which season did Aberdeen meet Helensburgh in the Scottish Cup? Also, what was the score?

629. In which season did Aberdeen meet Bo'ness in the Scottish Cup? Also, what was the score?

630. Which Aberdeen manager transferred Arthur Graham to Leeds United?

631. In which season did the Dons beat Celtic 6-2 at home and 5-1 away in League games?

632. Can you name the team Aberdeen defeated in a Scottish Cup tie 10-3 after a 2-2 draw?

633. Which Aberdeen manager has held this post for the least period of time?

634. Can you name all of Aberdeen's managers from 1903 to end of season 1985/86?

635. Can you name the club who purchased Aberdeen's old floodlights in 1970?

636. In which season did Aberdeen score a total of 38 goals in the League Cup competition, with only 12 against?

637. In which season did Hamilton Accies knock Aberdeen out of the semi-final of the Scottish Cup?

638. In which season did Aberdeen meet Arbroath in the semi-final of the Scottish Cup?

639. While a Dons player, Ally Shewan had an unbroken run of how many first team games?

640. Can you name Aberdeen's top goal scorer in season 1932/33?

Quiz 37
Questions 641-660

641. A record crowd of 16,000 turned up at Pittodrie on 20 January 1905—what was the occasion?

642. During the close season 1952/53, Aberdeen signed which player from Morton for a fee of £10,000?

643. Can you name the Aberdeen coach who resigned in January 1967?

644. Against which club did Ally Shewan make his 250th consecutive first team appearance for the Dons?

645. In season 1970/71 in the Cup Winners Cup competition, can you name the Aberdeen players who scored in the penalty shoot-out v Honved?

646. How many European goals did Drew Jarvie score while a Dons player?

647. Against which club did Martin Buchan score his first and only European goal for the Dons?

648. How many European goals did Dave Robb score while a Dons player?

649. In which season did Aberdeen draw only one League game?

650. In which season did Aberdeen lose only three League games?

651. Can you name the Aberdeen player of the 1960s who was known as "Jinky"?

652. In League games up to the end of season 1985/86, in which season did Aberdeen have the most goals scored against them?

653. Since Aberdeen Football Club first started competing in European competitions, which Aberdeen player has made most appearances for the Dons in Europe up to end of season 1985/86?

654. While a Dons player, in how many European games did Steve Archibald play?

655. Can you name the only Aberdeen player to score a goal in Dons European games, season 1977/78?

656. Can you name the Dons player(s) who scored in Aberdeen's first European game?

657. Against which club did Derek McKay make his only European appearance for the Dons?

658. Before hanging up his boots for good, Dons star of the 1950s, Don Emery, played for which Highland club, scoring 49 goals in one season?

659. Can you name the four Aberdeen players who scored their first European goal(s) for the Dons during the European Cup competition, season 1985/86?

660. How many European goals did Ian Hair score for the Dons in European competitions?

Quiz 38
Questions 661-680

661. In January 1985, the Dons played a friendly in Egypt. Can you name the club they played against? Also, what was the final score?

662. In what year did George Murray make his first appearance in the Dons first team?

663. What is Joey Harper's full name?

664. What is the least number of points Aberdeen have ended up with since the Premier League came into being? (To the end of season 1985/86).

665. Can you name the Dons player who scored the Dons first five goals in their 6-2 win over Airdrie at Brockville on 12 October 1957?

666. Against which club did Dave Robb make his 150th first team appearance for the Dons? Also, in which season?

667. In which year did Chic McLelland join Aberdeen Football Club?

668. Against which club and in which season did Billy Little make his first team debut for the Dons?

669. Against which club did Frank McDougall score his first hat trick for the Dons?

670. In which year did Archie Glen make his first team debut for the Dons?

671. Which Aberdeen player scored a hat trick v Alloa in the Scottish Cup third round, season 1984/85?

Picture Quiz 11
Signed by Aberdeen FC in 1972–had his testimonial game v Ipswich Town in August 1982?

672. Can you name the only native Aberdonian in the Dons team which won the Premier League championship in season 1979/80?

673. What was the fee Manchester United paid Aberdeen for Martin Buchan in 1972?

674. How many European games did Martin Buchan play for Aberdeen Football Club?

675. What was Aberdeen's final League placing and points total—season 1929/30?

676. How many Scottish caps did Dons star of the 1930s, Willie Mills, get in his time at Aberdeen?

677. Can you name the only Aberdeen player to score a goal in the European Cup, season 1980/81?

678. Can you name the player who was released at his own request by Aberdeen in December 1970? In his seven years at Pittodrie, he gained two under-23 caps.

679. Against which club did Andy Harrow score his first Premier goal for the Dons?

680. Can you name the player Aberdeen bought from Muggiemoss in 1927 for a fee of £20? This player spent 21 years at Pittodrie before being freed by the club in 1948.

Quiz 39
Questions 681-700

681. In season 1916/17, can you name the only Aberdeen player to play in all 38 League games?

682. Can you name the only Aberdeen player who appeared in all League games, season 1908/09?

683. Can you name the player who joined Aberdeen from Aston Villa in December 1908?

684. Can you name Aberdeen's top goal scorers in League games only in season 1914/15?

685. In which season were Aberdeen Football Club fined for failing to fulfil a fixture, even though the train carrying the Aberdeen players became snowbound at Forfar?

686. Can you name the Aberdeen player who, in his first full game for the Dons since his return from America, scored a hat trick v Dundee at Pittodrie in November 1980?

687. Can you name the club that were Aberdeen's opponents when the Pittodrie floodlights were switched on for the first time?

688. Can you name the Dons keeper deputising for John Ogston when the floodlights were first switched on at Pittodrie?

689. On how many occasions have Aberdeen met Stirling Albion in the Scottish Cup to the end of season 1985/86?

690. On how many occasions have the Dons met Cowdenbeath in the Scottish Cup to the end of season 1985/86?

691. On how many occasions have Aberdeen met Elgin City in the Scottish Cup to the end of season 1985/86?

692. In which season did the Dons last meet Queen's Park in the Scottish Cup to the end of season 1985/86?

693. Against which club did Frank McDougall make his first Scottish Cup appearance for the Dons?

694. Can you name the Aberdeen player who scored a hat trick in the Drybrough Cup v Airdrie, season 1980/81?

695. Against which club did keeper Marc De Clerck make his debut for the Dons?

696. Can you name the ex-Dons player who quit as manager of Forfar Athletic after only five days of accepting the post in August 1980?

697. Can you name the Yugoslav international striker who arrived at Pittodrie for a trial period in August 1980?

698. Can you name the player Aberdeen signed from Luton Town for £65,000 in January 1981?

699. Against which club did Andy Harrow score his first goal for the Dons?

700. Can you name the former Dons player who resigned as manager of Cowdenbeath in August 1980?

Quiz 40
Questions 701-720

701. Can you name the player Aberdeen signed from Manchester United in season 1949/50, who later joined Oldham Athletic in 1952?

702. In which season did the Dons first take part in the European Cup?

703. How many Scottish Cup goals did Steve Archibald score while he was playing for the Dons?

704. How many Scottish Cup goals did George Hamilton score for the Dons between 1938 and 1954?

705. Who scored the most Scottish Cup goals for the Dons up to the end of season 1985/86?

706. Who scored the most League goals for Aberdeen in season 1919/20?

707. Which Aberdeen player joined Everton in early 1920 for a fee of £1,500?

708. Which Aberdeen player has scored the most Scottish Cup goals in any one season up to the end of season 1985/86?

709. Only three Aberdeen players have scored five goals in any one Scottish Cup tie. Can you name them?

710. Can you name the Aberdeen player who scored a hat trick v Rangers in a Scottish Cup tie, season 1953-54?

711. Can you name the Aberdeen player who scored a hat trick in a Scottish Cup tie v Motherwell, season 1952/53?

712. Can you name the last Aberdeen player to score four goals in a Scottish Cup tie, to the end of season 1985/86?

713. Who were Aberdeen's opponents in the quarter-final of the Scottish Cup in season 1984/85?

714. Can you name the team who, in a Premier League game, became the first team to pull back a two-goal deficit, and force a 2-2 draw, during Alex Ferguson's reign as manager of the Dons?

715. Can you name the two Aberdeen players who were on the

Picture Quiz 12
Born in Edinburgh and signed from Seton Athletic in December 1968–but was not called up until July 1969–made his first-team debut for the Dons v Dundee at Dens Park on 5 September 1970?

Picture Quiz 13
This player was signed from Morton for a fee in the region of £10,000 during close season of 1952/53?

short list for the Scottish Football Writers' Player of the Year Award, season 1980/81?

716. What is the smallest crowd Aberdeen have ever played in front of in a European competition—to end of season 1985/86?

717. Up to the end of season 1985/86, what is the highest number of games Aberdeen have lost in any one season since the Premier League began?

718. Up the end of season 1985/86, what is the highest amount of goals Aberdeen have had scored against them in any one season since the Premier League began?

719. What is the lowest position Aberdeen have ever finished in the Premier League, to the end of season 1985/86?

720. In which season did Aberdeen first win the Premier League Championship?

Quiz 41
Questions 721-740

721. Can you name the first Aberdeen player to score a hat trick in a Scottish Cup tie?

722. Can you name the Aberdeen player who scored a hat trick in a Scottish Cup tie v Inverness Caley in season 1950/51?

723. Against which club did Ian Angus make his Premier League debut for the Dons?

724. Against which club did Alex McLeish make his Premier League debut for the Dons?

725. During season 1952/53, how many games did Aberdeen play before registering their first win?

726. Where was John McMaster born?

727. Where was Brian Mitchell born?

728. In the Aberdeen playing staff of season 1985/86, only three players were born in Aberdeen. Can you name them?

729. In 1979 Aberdeen signed two players from St Mirren. Can you name them?

730. Can you name the Aberdeen player who was their top scorer in seasons 1911/12, 1912/13, 1913/14, 1915/16?

731. What was the final league placing of Aberdeen Football Club in season 1960/61?

732. In which season did Aberdeen take part in a Scottish Cup final which attracted a record crowd for a club match in Britain?

733. Aberdeen Football Club made an offer of £150,000, which was rejected by Airdrie, for which player?

734. Can you name the only Aberdeen players to score in the European Cup in season 1984/85? (Not including penalty shoot-out.)

735. Can you name the only two Aberdeen players to score a goal in the UEFA Cup, season 1971/72?

736. Seven Aberdeen players scored their first goal for Aberdeen Football Club in a European competition against the same club. Can you name the players and the club in question?

737. In which European competition did the Dons take part in season 1968/69?

738. Can you name the Aberdeen player who made his European debut for the Dons v Eintracht Frankfurt in season 1979/80?

739. Who was Aberdeen's top goal scorer in season 1922/23?

740. In what position did Aberdeen finish in the League, season 1956/57?

Quiz 42
Questions 741-760

741. Can you name the former Aberdeen player who, after a spell with Leeds United, was transferred to Hearts in early 1985?

742. Which former Aberdeen manager was manager of Mother-well when the Dons beat them 8-0 at Pittodrie in a Premier League game?

743. Can you name the Aberdeen player who scored a hat-trick v Hibs at Easter Road in a Premier League game in 1985?

744. Can you name three Northern Ireland internationalists who have played for Aberdeen Football Club?

745. Can you name two Republic of Ireland internationalists who have played for Aberdeen Football Club?

746. In 1970 Aberdeen had two full international goalkeepers on their books at the same time. Can you name them?

747. While an Aberdeen player, how many full Scottish caps did Jock Hutton get?

748. While a Dons player, how many full international caps did Dave Robb get?

749. During 1955 Aberdeen had on their books Scotland's full international goalkeeper and Scotland's under-23 keeper. Can you name both keepers?

750. Can you name the team who knocked Aberdeen out of the Scottish Cup in season 1912/13?

751. In which position did Aberdeen Football Club finish in the League in season 1927/28?

752. Can you give the year a cover was first built over the King Street end at Pittodrie?

753. In which year were the Executive boxes first constructed at Pittodrie?

754. Can you name the two Aberdeen players who appear on the front cover of the publication *Here We Go*?

755. Can you name the ferry which took the Aberdeen supporters to Sweden for the European Cup Winners Cup final in season 1982/83?

756. In which season did Dundee United fail to score a single goal v Aberdeen in Premier League games?

757. Can you name the former Inverness Caley boot boy the Dons signed as a 16-year-old in April 1985?

758. Since the Premier League began, on how many occasions have Aberdeen defeated Hibs by 5 goals to 0, to the end of season 1985/86?

759. What is Aberdeen's highest win over St Mirren since the Premier League began, to the end of season 1985/86?

760. On how many occasions have the Dons scored five goals v Dundee since the Premier League began, to the end of season 1985/86?

Quiz 43

Questions 761-780

761. In which season did Aberdeen beat Morton in a Premier League game 6-0?

762. Only one Aberdeen player has scored a hat-trick v Morton since the Premier League began to the end of season 1985/86. Can you name the player?

763. Can you name the team Alex Ferguson played for as a teenager who were relegated in 1962?

764. While manager of Aberdeen Football Club, to the end of season 1983/84, can you name all the honours Alex Ferguson has taken to Pittodrie?

765. Between 23 January 1982 and March 1985, how many Scottish Cup games did Aberdeen play without a defeat?

766. On how many occasions did Rangers beat Aberdeen in Premier League games in season 1984/85?

767. Against which club did Neale Cooper make his 200th appearance for Aberdeen Football Club?

768. Before joining the Dons in 1969, can you name the clubs Jim Smith played for?

769. In which season since World War Two did Dumbarton play their first game at Pittodrie?

770. Can you name the skipper of the Aberdeen team who first won the Scottish Cup?

771. Can you name two Dons players who made their first team debut in season 1966/67, and made their 200th first team appearance in a midweek game v Queens Park in season 1972/73?

772. Can you name the former Aberdeen player who part-wrote the screen play *Keeping Up*?

773. In 1967 Aberdeen played two cup ties in Dundee, and both were played on the same ground. What were the results and the teams involved?

774. A former Newcastle United player played in goal for the Dons

in the early 60s, and a former "Geordie" managed the Club. Can you name them?

775. For which Dundee player did Aberdeen pay a then club record fee of £43,000?

776. In which season(s) did Aberdeen Football Club not compete in the Scottish League championship?

777. Can you name the Dons player sent off in the Scottish Cup semi-final replay v Dundee United in season 1984/85?

778. What was the score on the occasion when the Dons met Newcastle United in the Coronation Cup in 1953?

779. In which year did the Dons first meet Dundee United in a Scottish Cup game?

780. In which season did Dundee United first beat the Dons in a Scottish Cup match?

Quiz 44
Questions 781-800

781. In which season did Aberdeen last get a bye in the Scottish Cup?

782. In which season(s) did Aberdeen get a third-round bye in the Scottish Cup?

783. Has any Aberdeen player ever scored a hat trick for Scotland? If so, name the year and the player?

784. Who scored most goals for Aberdeen in Scottish Cup games, season 1984/85?

785. What was the lowest attendance at any of Aberdeen's games in the Scottish Cup, season 1984/85?

786. Which player substituted John Hewitt in the Scottish Cup semi-final replay v Dundee United, season 1984/85?

787. Which player substituted Dougie Bell in the Scottish Cup semi-final replay v Dundee United, season 1984/85?

788. On how many occasions during Premier League games in season 1984/85, did Aberdeen beat Dumbarton?

Picture Quiz 14
This Hungarian Internationalist was perhaps the most gifted player for the Dons in the 70's—signed from Hertha Berlin?

789. Towards the end of 1981, Aberdeen were unsuccessful in getting the services of which Belgian-based player?

790. In what year did Pittodrie have its first 32,000-plus crowd?

791. In which year did Pittodrie have its first 45,000-plus crowd?

792. In which season did Aberdeen beat Forfar 6-0 in a Scottish Cup game at Pittodrie?

793. Can you name the Austrian first division leading scorer Aberdeen showed an interest in signing in late 1981?

794. Can you name the two Dons players who were in Scotland's under-21 team who beat Italy 1-0 in February 1982?

795. When was the first time that Aberdeen Football Club won the League Championship in front of their own fans at Pittodrie?

796. Who scored the goal that clinched the Premier League championship for Aberdeen in season 1984/85?

797. Can you name the player Aberdeen signed from Motherwell for a then club record fee of £2,000 in 1923?

798. Which English club provided the opposition for Jock Hutton's Benefit at the end of season 1923/24?

799. Against which club did Willie Miller make his 50th Scottish Cup appearance for Aberdeen Football Club?

800. Who scored the goal that clinched the very first League championship for Aberdeen Football Club?

Quiz 45
Questions 801-820

801. Can you name the captain of Aberdeen Football Club when they played in their very first Scottish Cup final?

802. What was Aberdeen's highest League defeat in season 1923/24? And against which club?

803. Who made most League appearances for Aberdeen Football Club in season 1923/24?

804. During season 1984/85 Willie Miller missed only two League appearances. Can you name the Dons opponents on those occasions?

805. Which Cup did the Young Dons win in season 1984/85?

806. Can you name the Aberdeen players who scored hat tricks in Premier League games in season 1984/85?

807. Did Aberdeen win, lose or draw their first two Premier League games in season 1981/82?

808. In the League Cup, season 1981/82, the Dons beat Berwick Rangers by what aggregate?

809. Can you name the scorers of Aberdeen's goals in the Scottish Cup final 1981/82?

810. How many Premier League goals did John Hewitt score for the Dons during season 1981/82?

811. How many Premier League goals did Andy Watson score for the Dons during season 1981/82?

812. Can you name the Aberdeen player who scored in 20 seconds in a Premier League game v Airdrie in August 1980?

813. Up to the end of season 1985/86, what is Aberdeen's heaviest European defeat?

814. What is the highest amount of goals that have been scored against Aberdeen in a European competition?

815. Aberdeen had an offer of £150,000 turned down by Bristol City for which player in March 1981?

816. Against which club did Andy Harrow score his first goal for Aberdeen?

817. During the Dons' tour of Canada in 1956, they beat a Canadian team 17-0. Can you name the team?

818. On how many occasions did Bryan Gunn play in goal for the Dons in Premier League games 1984/85?

819. Aberdeen acquired the services of Ernie Ewen on a free transfer from which club pre-season 1952/53?

820. Who made most first team appearances in Premier League games for the Dons, season 1984/85?

Quiz 46
Questions 821-840

821. Who scored most penalty goals for Aberdeen in Premier League games, season 1984/85?

822. Against which team did Aberdeen lose their only Premier League game at Pittodrie, season 1984/85?

823. What was the poorest attendance at a Dons game in the Premier League during season 1984/85?

824. Who were the Dons opponents when they last contested the Drybrough Cup Final?

825. Can you name the player Aberdeen transferred to Stoke City in season 1952/53?

826. Can you name the two Aberdeen players who were in the top three Scottish goal scorers in competitive matches during season 1985/86?

827. How many goals did Eric Black score for the Dons in competitive matches in season 1984/85?

828. What are Aberdeen's change strip colours?

829. Can you name the player Aberdeen transferred to St. Mirren in 1983?

830. Which team knocked the Dons out of the Scottish Cup in season 1980/81?

831. Can you name the goalkeeper the Dons borrowed from Dundee United for the Drew Jarvie Testimonial v Ipswich?

832. Can you name the goalkeeper who was freed by Middlesbrough, and played in goals for the Dons in a friendly v Stirling Albion in August 1982?

833. Against which country did Jim Leighton save a penalty in a World Cup qualifying match in May 1985?

834. Can you name the former Dons manager who took over as manager of East Fife in November 1981?

835. Who were the Dons opponents in the quarter-final of the Scottish Cup in season 1982/83?

836. Against which club did Frank McDougall make his very first appearance in the Aberdeen colours?

837. What was the occasion when the Dons played Leicester City away from home in August 1984?

838. Can you name the former Dons striker who was transferred from Hibs to Hamilton Accies in September 1984?

Picture Quiz 15
This Welshman joined the Dons from Swindon Town in 1948 and ended his Scottish
League career with East Fife in 1956?

839. On Saturday, 22 December 1984, the Dons were beaten 1-0 by Dundee United in a League game. Previous to this, who were the last team to beat the Dons in a home League game?

840. On 12 January 1985, the Dons switched their League game with Morton from Cappielow to Pittodrie—for what reason?

Quiz 47
Questions 841-860

841. Can you name the three players Aberdeen Football Club were willing to consider offers for at the end of season 1984/85?

842. Can you name the former Aberdeen captain who emigrated to South Africa in 1938?

843. Can you name the Aberdeen player who scored a hat trick in the first half in a Premier League game v Hearts at Tynecastle in May 1985?

844. During season 1984/85 Tommy McQueen played in all the Dons Premier League games—except one. Who were the Dons opponents on this occasion?

845. Can you name the player the Dons signed from Falkirk in July 1985 for a fee in the region of £80,000?

846. Which country did Aberdeen Football Club tour pre-season 1985-86?

847. During the Dons pre-season tour of 1985/86, Aberdeen played a team they beat on aggregate 11-1 in a European competition. Can you name the team in question?

848. Can you name the Aberdeen player who was transferred to Hibs in August 1985?

849. Against which club did Jim Bett make his first Premier League appearance for the Dons?

850. Against which club did Willie Miller make his 700th first team appearance for the Dons?

851. How many first team appearances did Steve Cowan make for the Dons?

852. Against which club and in which competition did Steve Gray make his first team debut in competitive football for the Dons?

853. Can you name the four Dons players who were in the Scotland squad for the World Cup qualifying match v Wales at Cardiff in September 1985?

854. Against which club, and in which competition did Steve Gray make his European debut for the Dons?

855. Which English club were the Dons opponents for Jimmy Smith's benefit game in October 1929?

856. In the 1929/30 Scottish Cup the Dons drew 3-3 away from home, but won the replay 7-0 at home against which club?

857. In which competition did Steve Gray score his first goal for the Dons in a first team game?

858. Against which club did John Hewitt score his first European goal for the Dons?

859. Can you name the former Aberdeen player who was national coach for Australia during the World Cup qualifying games in 1985?

860. Can you name the player who came on for Eric Black in the European Cup first round, first leg v Akranes in September 1985?

Quiz 48
Questions 861-880

861. Which Aberdeen player was transferred to Rangers in August 1985?

862. Against which club did Jim Bett score his first Premier League goal for the Dons?

863. Can you state the fee involved between Hibs and Aberdeen for the transfer of Steve Cowan?

864. Can you name the Dons player who was booked in the opening minutes of the Scotland v Wales game in September 1985?

865. Against which club did Billy Stark score his first European goal for the Dons?

866. In which month and year was the new Merkland Stand first used, and who was the visiting team on this occasion?

867. Against which club did Steve Gray score his first Premier League goal for the Dons?

868. Which Aberdeen player made his 400th first team appearance for the Dons v Hibs at Easter Road on 12 October 1985?

869. Against which club did Willie Falconer score his first European goal for the Dons?

870. Can you name the Aberdeen player Blackpool signed from the Dons in season 1933/34 for a fee in the region of £3,000?

871. Where did Aberdeen Football Club tour in season 1932/33?

872. On 17 March 1951, Aberdeen reserves gave which club their record defeat?

873. In the Scottish Cup of 1889/90, Aberdeen lost 13-1 to which team?

874. From which club did Aberdeen sign Steve Beckett?

875. Which former Aberdeen player was appointed coach of Floriana (Malta) in 1952?

876. What was the fee Rangers paid Aberdeen for the services of Doug Bell?

877. How many first team appearances did Doug Bell make for the Dons?

878. On leaving Pittodrie, Neil Cooper played for two English Clubs before joining St. Mirren. Can you name the clubs?

879. Can you name the former Dons player who resigned as manager of Burnley after only 110 days in 1985?

880. Against which club did Frank McDougall make his first European appearance for the Dons?

Quiz 49
Questions 881-900

881. Can you name the scorer(s) of Aberdeen's goal(s) in the Skol League Cup final in October 1985?

Picture Quiz 16
Manchester United paid Aberdeen a fee of £125,000 in March 1971 for the services of this player?

882. In the Skol League Cup competition 1985/86, how many goals did Aberdeen have scored against them?

883. On what occasion did John Hewitt make his 200th first team appearance for the Dons?

884. Can you name the player Aberdeen signed from Campsie Black Watch in October 1985?

885. Can you name the Aberdeen player who scored four goals against Celtic in a Premier League game in November 1985?

886. Can you name the major competition Aberdeen Football Club won on a Sunday?

887. In post-war games, only two Aberdeen players have scored four goals v Celtic in one game. Can you name both players?

888. In a Premier League game at Pittodrie in December 1985 v Hibs, can you name three Dons players who scored their first Premier League goals of the season?

889. Can you name the Dons Scottish internationalist who was born in England?

890. Against which club did Billy Stark score his 50th goal for the Dons?

891. What Premier Division record did Frank McDougall equal during season 1984/85?

892. Can you name another Scottish League side which was founded in the same year as Aberdeen Football Club?

893. During season 1940/41, can you name the club who played all their home games at Pittodrie?

894. Prior to their Scottish Cup meeting in season 1985/86, when last did Montrose meet Aberdeen in a Scottish Cup tie?

895. Can you name the only Aberdeen player to score a hat trick v Dundee in a Premier League game up to the end of season 1985/86?

896. How many goals did St. Johnstone score against the Dons in Premier League games in season 1983/84?

897. Can you name the Aberdeen Secretary who resigned in January 1976?

898. Can you name the player Aberdeen signed from Kilmarnock in December 1975?

899. Can you name the former Aberdeen mid-field player who signed for Berwick Rangers in January 1986?

900. Which trophy did Aberdeen Football Club win in January 1986?

Quiz 50
Questions 901-920

901. How many managers did Aberdeen Football Club have during the 70s?

902. Can you name the only Aberdeen player to score against Dundee United in Premier League games in season 1977/78?

903. What was the admission charge for entry into the Paddock for the Aberdeen v Liverpool European Cup, second round tie in 1980?

904. On 3 August 1983, the Dons played against local side Cove Rangers in a friendly. What was the score?

905. Can you name Aberdeen's top goal scorers (in any one season) during the 1950s League games/Scottish Cup/League Cup games only?

906. Can you name the Aberdeen player who scored six goals v Falkirk on 14 September 1932?

907. Two Aberdeen players scored 30 goals each in League/Scottish Cup games in season 1936/37, can you name them?

908. How many under-21 caps has John Hewitt, to end of season 1985/86?

909. Can you name Aberdeen Football Club's top goal scorer for one season?

910. Against which club did Bryan Gunn make his European debut for the Dons?

911. Can you name the Aberdeen player who made his 50th European appearance for the Dons v FK Gothenburg at Pittodrie in March 1986?

912. In season 1914/15, Aberdeen's top goal scorers scored only eight goals each. Can you name the players in question?

913. Dave Shaw resigned as manager of Aberdeen following a Cup Final defeat by which club?

914. Can you name two Aberdeen players who were in the Scotland side v Norway on 19 May 1954?

915. In 18 years of football, on how many occasions was George Hamilton (Gentleman George) booked?

916. Can you name the Aberdeen player who scored a hat trick v Clydebank in a Premier League game on 8 February 1986?

917. Can you name the Aberdeen player who was transferred to Swindon in 1948 in a deal which took Don Emery to Pittodrie?

918. In which year did Aberdeen first play a League game at Tannadice?

919. How many Aberdeen players scored a goal in both Scottish Cup and League Cup, and at least one goal in League games during season 1975/76?

920. Which club did Dons star of the 40s and 50s, George Hamilton, end his career with?

Quiz 51
Questions 921-940

921. Joe Harper was once a signed Liverpool player. TRUE/ FALSE?

922. The present-day capacity of Pittodrie is 27,000. TRUE/ FALSE?

923. Dave Halliday was the very first Aberdeen manager. TRUE/FALSE?

924. Aberdeen won the Scottish Cup in 1947. TRUE/FALSE?

925. The Dons won the Drybrough Cup in 1971 and 1978. TRUE/FALSE?

926. On leaving Pittodrie, Ally McLeod became Scotland's manager. TRUE/FALSE?

927. Aberdeen Football Club first became League Champions in 1954/55. TRUE/FALSE?

Picture Quiz 17
This man was responsible for taking such talents as Gordon Strachan and Steve Archibald to Pittodrie?

Picture Quiz 18
This is the Aberdeen Scottish Cup winning side of which year?

928. Alex Ferguson took over at Pittodrie in June 1977.
     TRUE/FALSE?

929. Aberdeen Football Club were originally known as Banks o'
     Dee. TRUE/FALSE?

930. The Dons signed Ally Shewan from local side Formartine
     United. TRUE/FALSE?

931. Before signing for the Dons, Doug Rougvie played for
     Dunfermline Athletic. TRUE/FALSE?

932. Joe Harper was the first Aberdeen player to win the Footballer
     of the Year Award. TRUE/FALSE?

933. Dons player of the 70s, Zoltan Varga, was banned from
     playing football in West Germany because of a bribery
     scandal. TRUE/FALSE?

934. George Mulhall was the only Aberdeen player to get a
     Scottish cap between 1958-1966. TRUE/FALSE?

935. Celtic knocked Aberdeen out of the League Cup in season
     1983/84. TRUE/FALSE?

936. Mark McGhee signed for the Dons in April 1978.
     TRUE/FALSE?

937. Neil Simpson had trials with Nottingham Forest before
     signing for the Dons. TRUE/FALSE?

938. Albion Rovers have never defeated Aberdeen in a Scottish
     Cup game. TRUE/FALSE?

939. Arthur Graham won a Scottish Cup winners medal within
     four months of becoming a Dons player. TRUE/FALSE?

940. During a tour of America in 1967, Aberdeen Football Club
     were known as "Washington Whips". TRUE/FALSE?

Quiz 52
Questions 941-960

941. Can you name the former Aberdeen manager who had the
     novel idea of the Dons travelling to away games by charter
     plane?

942. Which team did Aberdeen defeat in the final of the Mitchell Trophy in season 1944/45?

943. In the second series of the North Eastern League, season 1944/45, what was Aberdeen's final League placing?

944. Four weeks prior to winning the Scottish Cup for the very first time, Aberdeen were defeated 4-0 by which team in the final of the League Cup?

945. In the North Eastern League in which the Dons participated during the war years, how were the points awarded?

946. Can you name the Aberdeen player who was in the Scottish side v Belgium at Hampden in January 1946?

947. Can you name the Aberdeen goalkeeper of the 50s who, if it was raining, did his Friday morning sprint carrying an umbrella?

948. Which club did Archie Baird join from the Dons in 1953?

949. During the reign of Dave Halliday as manager of Aberdeen—on how many occasions did Aberdeen reach the final of the Scottish Cup?

950. Which Aberdeen manager was known by the players as "Faither"?

951. In season 1941/42, Aberdeen beat Dundee United in the final of which two competitions?

952. In 1950 Aberdeen signed a player from Hibs. This player later became manager of Aberdeen. Can you name him?

953. Which former Aberdeen player was once headmaster of Hilton Academy, Aberdeen?

954. In what year did Pittodrie stage its first international game?

955. In what year was the ornamental granite façade erected at the Merkland Road end of Pittodrie?

956. Former Aberdeen manager, Eddie Turnbull, was a member of the greatest forward line in the history of Hibs. By what name were they better known?

957. Can you name Aberdeen's first £2,000 signing?

958. What was the admission charge to get into Pittodrie during season 1918/19?

959. In 1933 the Dons signed a player named Willie Gall from which club?

960. In November 1966, the then manager of Aberdeen, Eddie Turnbull, turned down an offer to manage which club?

Quiz 53
Questions 961-980

961. In their opening game in season 1933/34, Aberdeen defeated which team 8-0?

962. In the last game of the 1933/34 season v Queens Park, which Aberdeen player scored twice and then repeated this feat for the reserves in the same evening?

963. During season 1977/78, five new players were signed by Aberdeen. Can you name them?

964. Can you name Aberdeen's very first trainer?

965. Can you name the player who scored Aberdeen's very first goal?

966. Can you name the goalkeeper Aberdeen signed from Middlesbrough in 1904?

967. Can you name Aberdeen's opponents in their very first game in Scottish League football?

968. For which amateur side did former Dons player Doug Considine play during season 1985/86?

969. Bristol Rovers signed two Aberdeen players in May 1907. Can you name them?

970. Can you name the Aberdeen player who scored a hat-trick in a Scottish Cup tie v Queens Park, season 1907/08?

971. Against which club did Aberdeen win their only away League game during season 1916/17?

972. Can you name the former Inverurie Loco's keeper who played for Aberdeen in their early years?

973. Can you name the player Aberdeen Football Club signed from Newcastle United in season 1908/09?

Picture Quiz 19
This player was signed for Aberdeen by Dave Halliday for a fee in the region of £3,000
from Queen of the South in the late 30's–he also scored a hat-trick for Scotland v Belgium
in 1951–pictured with another Dons star of the same era?

974. In 1914 an Aberdeen player expressed a desire to leave the club, and his transfer fee was set at £200 by the Scottish League. Can you name the player in question?

975. In what season did Aberdeen finish at the foot of Division One?

976. Which Aberdeen player from season 1912/13 to 1915/16 was Aberdeen's top scorer?

977. Against which club did Joe Miller score his first Scottish Cup goal for the Dons?

978. In which year did Arbroath knock Aberdeen out of the Scottish Cup in the first round?

979. In which season was Dave Robb top goal scorer for the Dons?

980. What was Aberdeen's final League placing in season 1963/64?

Quiz 54
Questions 981-1001

981. By what name was Aberdeen keeper Alex Mutch known in the early years of Aberdeen Football Club?

982. Aberdeen scored no goals in the Scottish Cup in season 1964/65. TRUE/FALSE?

983. Floodlights were first installed at Pittodrie in 1953 to mark the Coronation. TRUE/FALSE?

984. Who was Aberdeen's top goal scorer in season 1926/27?

985. During seasons 1955/56, 1956/57, 1957/58, Aberdeen Football Club never played a Scottish Cup game at Pittodrie. TRUE/FALSE?

986. Can you name Aberdeen's goalkeeper in their very first Scottish Cup winning side?

987. Before becoming assistant manager at Pittodrie, Archie Knox was manager of Montrose Football Club. TRUE/FALSE?

988. When was the last time Aberdeen got a bye in the Scottish Cup?

989. What is the least amount of goals Aberdeen have scored in League games in any one season—to end of season 1985/86?

990. What is the highest amount of games (League) Aberdeen have lost in any one season, to the end of season 1985/86?

991. On how many occasions have Aberdeen Football Club received byes in the Scottish Cup?

992. For which Aberdeen Junior side did present-day trainer Teddy Scott play?

993. Can you name the very first player Alex Ferguson transferred from Aberdeen Football Club?

994. What was the duration of John Pattillo's stay as trainer at Pittodrie?

995. In his playing days, for which club(s) did ex-manager Jimmy Bonthrone play?

996. On how many occasions have East Fife knocked Aberdeen out of the Scottish Cup?

997. In January 1985 Aberdeen Football Club played a friendly in Sweden. TRUE/FALSE?

998. Ex Dons player Andy Watson was transferred to Hearts from Aberdeen. TRUE/FALSE?

999. What was the admission to the South Stand for League games during season 1985/86?

1000. Can you name the ex-Aberdeen manager who is at present commercial manager for East Fife?

1001. In the entire history of Aberdeen Football Club, they have only failed to score a goal in the Scottish Cup competition in two seasons. In which seasons did this happen?

Picture Quiz 20
This Fife born player was signed from junior club Dunfermline United in 1972–moved to
Chelsea under freedom of contact end of season 1983/84?

THE DONS' QUIZ BOOK

Answers

ANSWERS

Quiz 1

1. Arthur Graham.
2. Martin Buchan (Aberdeen).
3. Twice.
4. 13-0 v Peterhead.
5. Scottish Cup, 3rd round, 10 February 1923.
6. Alex Cheyne, Aberdeen; Hampden; 13 April 1929; Scotland v England, 88th minute.
7. Aberdeen 6 Rangers 0.
8. Dunfermline United.
9. 1976.
10. 12 times: 1936/37; 1946/47; 1952/53; 1953/54; 1958/59; 1966/67; 1969/70; 1977/78; 1981/82; 1982/83; 1983/84; 1985/86.
11. Bumper.
12. 24,000.
13. Yes, 1917; then dropped out of League for two years.
14. 1907/08 v Celtic. Celtic won 1-0.
15. Season 1919/20. Albion Rovers won 2-1.
16. Notts County.
17. August 1972.
18. March 1978.
19. John Hewitt.
20. 12.

Quiz 2

21. Three times—1976/77, 1979/80, 1978/79.
22. Clark, Boel, Murray, Hermiston, McMillan, Buchan, McKay, Robb, Forrest, Harper, Graham.
23. 129,926. Aberdeen v Celtic.
24. Harper (pen.) McKay 2.
25. 1971—Celtic. 1980—St. Mirren.

26. 96—Season 1935/36.
27. A Gaelic word meaning "Hill of Dung".
28. Yes.
29. 1971 and 1980.
30. Ullevi Stadium, Gothenburg, Sweden.
31. 1903.
32. Celtic.
33. 1947.
34. Clyde.
35. Hibs.
36. 45,061 v Hearts; 13 March 1954.
37. Clark, Whyte, Shewan, Peterson, McMillan, M. Buchan, Wilson, Munro, Storrie, Smith, Taylor; 1967/68 Cup Winners Cup.
38. Dave Robb, Aberdeen, 93rd minute.
39. 3 May 1980 v Hibs. Aberdeen won 5-0.
40. Six times.

Quiz 3

41. Record attendance Glebe Park, Brechin, 8,123.
42. 1947; 1970; 1982; 1983; 1984; 1986.
43. Yes; Season 1904/05. Although finishing 7th in Division Two, they were promoted to Division One in Season 1905/06.
44. Goalkeeper John Ogston.
45. Johnstone, McKenna, Taylor, McLaughlin, Dunlop, Waddell, Harris, Hamilton, Williams, Baird, McColl.
46. 1967/68.
47. Aberdeen 10 KRR Reykjavik 0—European Cup Winners Cup 1967/68 at Pittodrie. Aberdeen won 14-1 on aggregte.
48. Steve Archibald (21 goals).
49. Pride of Aberdeen (Paul Ames 1980); Aberdeen c/w Wee Red Devils (Red Brigade 1983); Up the Dons (Robbie Shepherd 1983).
50. Quarter-finals, going down 1-0 to Celtic after a 0-0 draw.
51. Ally McLeod.
52. Stuart Kennedy, Ian Fleming, Joe Harper, Dom Sullivan, Jim Shirra.

53. Falkirk for £26,000.
54. Mark McGhee.
55. Season 1954/55.
56. Peterhead.
57. Rumania in Bucharest; June 1975.
58. Williams (Hamilton also scored).
59. Aberdeen, 1980.
60. Jim Forrest.

Quiz 4

61. April 1973 v Morton at Cappielow.
62. To take over as manager of Scotland.
63. Celtic. Aberdeen 3 Celtic 1.
64. Yes, twice. 1970/71 European Cup Winners Cup, having won first leg at Pittodrie 3-1 v Honved. Dons lost return leg 3-1. Honved won 5-4 on penalties. European Cup 1984/85 v Dynamo Berlin 3-3 on aggregate. Dynamo Berlin won 5-4 on penalties.
65. Peterhead. Aberdeenshire Cup Winners Medal 1971.
66. 7 April 1973 v Airdrie at Pittodrie. Aberdeen 5 Airdrie 1.
67. 1936/37 losing 2-1 to Celtic.
68. Yes, Season 1945/46, beating Rangers 3-2.
69. Season 1946/47, losing 4-0 to Rangers.
70. 0-8 v Celtic, Division One, 30 January 1965.
71. Season 1974/75, quarter-finals at Pittodrie. Motherwell won 1-0.
72. Eddie Thomson. Fee £65,000.
73. Joe Harper.
74. The Don.
75. Aberdeen v Honved. 1970/71 Cup Winners Cup.
76. Lech Poznan (Poland).
77. 1965.
78. Dave Smith.
79. Jimmy Wilson.
80. John McCormick and Tommy White.

Quiz 5

81. 1965.
82. Francis Munro.
83. Four. 2—Sion; 1—Waterschei; 1—Real Madrid.
84. June 1978.
85. 25.
86. 6.
87. Willie Miller; Scottish Cup 1982; 1983.
88. Yes. 1971/72—UEFA Cup, 2nd round, 2nd leg. 1-1. Juventus won 1st leg 2-0.
89. Marek Dimitrov. Aggregate score 6-2.
90. Yes. UEFA Cup, Season 1972/73, 2nd leg Borussia Moenchengladbach 6 Aberdeen 3. Aberdeen also lost 1st leg at Pittodrie 2-3.
91. Aberdeen 1 Dinamo Tirana 0. Goal scored at Pittodrie.
92. Yes, 1977/78. Rangers 2 Aberdeen 1.
93. Dave Shaw.
94. No.
95. Nine. Alex Ferguson is the 10th.
96. Jack Webster.
97. Jimmy Bonthrone.
98. Dick Donald; Ian Donald.
99. London; 15 November 1951.
100. Dalry Thistle.

Quiz 6

101. May 1978. Sheffield United.
102. Jimmy Philip. 1903/1924.
103. Charlie Cooke with Chelsea, 1971 v Real Madrid.
104. 18 March 1939.
105. 17 years. 1938-1955.
106. Stenhousemuir; 15 August 1903. Northern League.
107. July 1976.
108. Tommy Pearson.
109. White.

110. Willie Lennie. 1908.
111. Jimmy Philip. 21 years, 1903/1924.
112. 1977.
113. Juvenile side Glasgow United.
114. 75th.
115. Paddy Travers.
116. Black and Gold.
117. 68.
118. Drew Jarvie v Dundee, 2 February 1980; Ian Scanlon v Arbroath (Scottish Cup) 30 January 1980; Steve Archibald v Celtic (League Cup) 31 October 1979. Steve Archibald also scored 4 goals v Airdrie (Scottish Cup) 16 February 1980.
119. St. Mirren.
120. Arbroath.

Quiz 7

121. Dundee.
122. Falkirk (approximately £10,000).
123. Newburgh Juniors.
124. Dave Robb.
125. 1881.
126. Aberdeen FC—Orion—Victoria United.
127. 7, 3, 2, 4, 1, 2, 2, 3, 1, 1, 4.
128. 1960.
129. 6 February 1971.
130. Jimmy Bonthrone.
131. Jim Shirra.
132. Zoltan Varga.
133. John Hewitt, 9.7 seconds v Motherwell, 3rd round 1981/82. 23 January 1982.
134. Yes, 1969, while a Rangers player; however Rangers lost 4-0 to Celtic.
135. Won 216—drawn 101—lost 79.
136. 1966.
137. Borussia Moenchengladbach, 13 September 1972, 2-3.
138. Away 1-1, Home 3-1, Aggregate 4-2.
139. Gordon Strachan v Rangers, 1 September 1979.
140. Germany.

Quiz 8

141. For purposely fielding an understrength team v Queen's Park so that Queen's Park would avoid relegation.
142. Willie Lennie. £150.
143. Hugh McLaren. Aberdeen loaned him to Kilmarnock for cup games only.
144. Fred Martin.
145. £5 per week, plus £2 bonus for a win; £1 for a draw. By 1935 Dons players were on £7 per week, plus bonus.
146. Welshman Jackie Beynon died in a Johannesburg Hospital during tour, with peritonitis.
147. Martin Buchan, 1970.
148. Newcastle United, April 1904. Newcastle won 7-1.
149. Drew 1-1 v Stenhousemuir (Northern League).
150. Donald Colman (Cunningham).
151. Jock Hutton.
152. 1908 v Celtic. MacFarlane, Colman, Hume, Halkett, McIntosh, Low, McDonald, Muir, Murray, O'Hagen, Lennie.
153. Following a stone-throwing incident v Rangers.
154. Trainer's dugout.
155. Willie Cooper.
156. July 1947, from Annbank United.
157. February 1949 v Falkirk at Brockville.
158. Norway.
159. December 1948, Annfield Plain.
160. St. Johnstone.

Quiz 9

161. Darkie.
162. 110 yards x 71 yards.
163. Raith Rovers at Starks Park.
164. Paddy Wilson, 19 October 1966 v Rangers at Ibrox.
165. Gordon Strachan.
166. Three times—1953, 1954, 1959.
167. McGhee (1), Weir (1).

Picture Quiz 21
Former coach who was confirmed as boss of the Dons in August 1971, amongst his
signings Drew Jarvie and Jocky Scott?

168. St. Mirren.
169. Alec Young v Celtic.
170. Martin, Mitchell, Caldwell, Allister, Young, Glen, Leggat, Hamilton, Hather, Buckley, Clunie. Celtic won 2-1.
171. Leicester City.
172. Club trainer.
173. Jimmy Mitchell.
174. Harry Yorston.
175. Harry Yorston.
176. 1, 2, 5, 11, 13, 15.
177. Martin, Caldwell, Hogg, Brownlie, Clunie, Glen, Ewen, Davidson, Baird, Wishart, Hather.
178. St. Mirren 3 Aberdeen 1.
179. A loss of £13,000 and a bank overdraft of £12,000.
180. 17.

Quiz 10

181. Clark, Whyte, Shewan, Munro, McMillan, Peterson, Wilson, Smith, Storrie, Melrose, Johnstone.
182. Jens Peterson.
183. Washington Whips.
184. Willie Falconer v Waterschei.
185. Zoltan Varga.
186. 44,000.
187. Henning Boel.
188. Arthur Graham.
189. Jimmy Bonthrone.
190. 1959-1964.
191. Willie Young in 1972. Within a week he was transferred to Tottenham Hotspur for a fee of £100,000.
192. John Dick.

193. Ayr United.
194. Zoltan Varga.
195. Willie Young and Arthur Graham. Joe Harper was also banned but was with Everton at the time. Ban was lifted in 1977.
196. Tampa Bay Rowdies. 1978.
197. Ernie Winchester.
198. India.
199. 60,000 v SV Hamburg, UEFA Cup, 3rd round, 2nd leg.
200. Jimmy Bonthrone.

Quiz 11

201. 1982.
202. 24 times.
203. Ally Shewan.
204. 108,591.
205. Jim Clunie.
206. Andy Harrow, Andy Dornan.
207. Aberdeen: won 6; drawn 3.
208. Eric Black.
209. Hertha Berlin.
210. Aberdeen v Celtic.
211. £14 per week.
212. Martin Buchan. 1970/71.
213. Willie Garner, at the age of 27.
214. Eddie Thomson v Kilmarnock at Rugby Park.
215. Ally Shewan.
216. Lennie Taylor.
217. Blackwell, Hutton, Forsyth, MacLachlan, Milne, Robertson, Middleton, Thomson, Grant, Rankin, Smith.
218. Luton Town.
219. Ian Scanlon.
220. 6-0 v Morton, 6 September 1980, at Pittodrie.

Quiz 12

221. Morton, 4th round. 1-0.
222. 26.
223. Marc De Clerck v Berwick Rangers, 30 August 1980, while playing for Aberdeen.
224. 1935 William Henry Strauss; 1936 Herbert Currer; 1937 Pat Kelly; 1938 Alfred Stanley Williams.
225. April 1979.
226. A Mascanheras.
227. Eversley Lewis.
228. Newcastle United.
229. Noel Ward.
230. Joergen Ravn, Leif Mortensen.
231. Henning Boel; Jens Peterson.
232. Henning Boel.
233. Saturday, 8 September 1984 v Morton at Cappielow; 71 appearances as sub.
234. April 1976.
235. Matt Armstrong.
236. George Hamilton.
237. Partick Thistle at Firhill.
238. £56.12.11 in 1873.
239. None.
240. 1935, Scottish Cup v Celtic.

Quiz 13

241. Ujpest Dozsa, quarter-finals European Cup Winners Cup, 1st leg, 7 March 1984.
242. Duns, 1954, at Duns.
243. Jimmy Philip, 1903-1924.
244. Wisla Krakow.
245. 5-0 Aberdeen.
246. They both played for Falkirk.
247. 5-1 Aberdeen.
248. August 1981.

249. Forfar Athletic.
250. Pat Stanton.
251. 7 points. Celtic 56 points; Aberdeen 49 points.
252. Queen of the South at Pittodrie.
253. Leith Athletic at Pittodrie.
254. 15 points. 3rd, Aberdeen—53 points. 4th, Rangers—38 points.
255. None. Celtic and Aberdeen had 53 points each, but Celtic had the better goal difference.
256. 5th.
257. Dundee.
258. George Buchan.
259. Steve Murray.
260. Tommy Rae.

Quiz 14

261. Ipswich Town.
262. Tottenham Hotspur.
263. Celtic Vigo.
264. 5.
265. 1910/11.
266. Benny Yorston, 38 goals.
267. Neil Simpson.
268. 115.
269. Played 67, won 32, drew 16, lost 19.
270. Three—Ipswich, Liverpool, Tottenham.
271. One v Hibs at Easter Road, 30 October 1982.
272. John Hewitt.
273. 12th out of 16 clubs, season 1905/06.
274. Partick Thistle at Pittodrie.
275. Kilmarnock, 2-0 at Pittodrie, September 1905.
276. November 1946.
277. Joe Harper, 197 goals.
278. The Wasps.
279. Partick Thistle, 4-2.
280. Two.

Quiz 15

281. None.
282. Hibs 4-1, Dundee 1-0, Partick Thistle 2-1, Celtic 1-0, Rangers 1-0.
283. Beaten finalists.
284. Joe Harper, Bobby Clark, Stuart Kennedy.
285. 1978.
286. 1973, from Hurlford.
287. Benny Yorston.
288. Harry Yorston.
289. Martin, Caldwell, Hogg, Brownlie, Clunie, Glen, Ewen, Davidson, Baird, Wishart, Hather.
290. Norman Davidson.
291. East Fife.
292. Bobby Clark.
293. 1969.
294. Archie Glen.
295. Fred Martin.
296. March 1908 v Celtic.
297. Norman Davidson
298. Francis Munro, 1967/68. Cup Winners Cup v KRR Reykjavik.
299. Geoghagan v Celtic Vigo, 1971/72, and v Borussia Moenchengladbach 1972/73. Bryan Gunn v IFK Gothenburg 1985/86.
300. 1978/79, Cup Winners Cup v Marek Dimitrov.

Quiz 16

301. 344.
302. Dave Halliday.
303. Ally McLean.
304. Eddie Thomson.
305. Willie Miller.
306. Alan Lyons, 16 years of age.
307. Bobby Calder.
308. Miller, McLeish. Standby—Jim Leighton.

309. Celtic 2-1 at Parkhead 6 October 1984.
310. Martin Buchan.
311. Hibs 0 Aberdeen 5, 3 May 1980.
312. 3 times, drew 1.
313. Martin, goalkeeper.
314. Clyde.
315. Season 1952/53. Rangers 1 Aberdeen 0, after a 1-1 draw.
316. Drew Jarvie Testimonial.
317. Only once—v Dundee United at Tannadice, November 1975.
318. Jim Storrie.
319. Falkirk.
320. 7,217 v Morton, 6 February 1982.

Quiz 17

321. Jim Leighton missed no League games in season 1981/82.
322. Tottenham Hotspur.
323. 274 plus 34 as sub.
324. Hugh McLaren, although a signed Aberdeen player, was on loan to Kilmarnock when they won the Scottish Cup v Rangers in 1929.
325. August 1980, Drybrough Cup. Aberdeen won 2-1.
326. 6 Scottish Cup games; 4 League Cup games.
327. 3 April 1982 v St. Mirren.
328. Billy Stark.
329. Jim Clunie.
330. Arges Pitesti, UEFA Cup, 2nd round, 1st leg, 21 October 1981.
331. Liverpool.
332. St. Mungo's Cup. Were beaten in final by Celtic.
333. Gordon Strachan v Dundee; Pittodrie; 20 August 1983.
334. 4.
335. 183.
336. Celtic 8 Aberdeen 0; Parkhead; 30 January 1965.
337. Donald Colman.
338. Gentleman George.
339. Fred Martin, goalkeeper, 1954.
340. Airdrie. Dons won 4-1.

Quiz 18

341. Raith Rovers at Pittodrie; League Cup, 2nd round, 24 August 1983.
342. Raith Rovers at Pittodrie; League Cup, 2nd round, 24 August 1983.
343. 8-0 v Airdrie at Pittodrie; Scottish Cup, 4th round, 16 February 1980.
344. Only 5. Because of war, SFA officially declared season 1939/40 null and void.
345. FC Twente '65' Enschede.
346. v Dundee, 20 August 1983.
347. 3.
348. Matt Armstrong v Celtic, 1937.
349. Dunfermline Athletic, East End Park.
350. Willie Mills.
351. Ally Shewan.
352. George Mulhall.
353. 7.
354. Fred Martin, Bobby Clark, Jim Leighton, Ernie McGarr.
355. 4.
356. 9-0 v Raith Rovers at Pittodrie; League Cup, 2nd round, 1st leg, 24 August 1983.
357. Two v Dundee and Celtic.
358. 3-1 v Dundee United, Pittodrie, quarter-final.
359. 65,529 approximately.
360. Dundee United—4-1 aggregate.

Quiz 19

361. Won 4-1 v Morton, 4 September 1983.
362. 11.
363. Eric Black.
364. 6.
365. Gordon Strachan, 7.
366. Bell.
367. Waterschei 1-0, semi-final.

Picture Quiz 22
Signed by Eddie Turnbull from Bonnyrigg Rose in 1965–was the choice of the Scottish Professional Footballers Association as their player of the year season 1973/74?

Picture Quiz 23
Known as "Tubby" Aberdeen sold this goalkeeper to Liverpool for a fee of £12,000 in 1965?

368. 30.
369. Mark McGhee.
370. 10. McGhee, Hewitt, Strachan, Black, Simpson, Kennedy, Weir, Bell, McLeish.
371. Hewitt for Simpson v Bayern Munich; Hewitt for Black v Waterschei; Weir for Black v Sion; also Hewitt for Black v Real Madrid.
372. Joe Harper.
373. Queen's Park.
374. 1965/66.
375. Rangers.
376. Sheffield Wednesday.
377. Wales.
378. 13.
379. Third Lanark.
380. Hamilton.

Quiz 20

381. Aberdeen won 5-0.
382. 351.
383. Kilmarnock.
384. Muirton Park, Perth.
385. Clyde at Pittodrie, 4-0.
386. Knattspyrnufelag Reykjavikur (KRR Reykjavik FC).
387. Harry Melrose.
388. Sparta Rotterdam.
389. Dens Park, Dundee.
390. Nijmegen.
391. Aberdeen 2 Eintracht 3.
392. 1955, Aberdeen won 4-3; 1967, Aberdeen won 2-1.
393. Jim Whyte.
394. John Craig.
395. Jim Henry.
396. Banks of Dee "A".
397. Kilbirnie Ladeside.

398. Edina.
399. Wee Alickie.
400. 1972.

Quiz 21

401. 6.
402. Aberdeen 5 Elgin City 0.
403. None.
404. 1969.
405. A. Smith; Alex Willoughby.
406. Aberdeen 6 Falkirk 0, March 1974.
407. Mark McGhee (2).
408. 3.
409. 61 points.
410. Final, but lost to Wolves.
411. 1967 in America.
412. Penalty by Archie Glen v Clyde, 9 April 1955.
413. 9 April 1955 v Clyde at Shawfield. Aberdeen won 1-0.
414. 8-0 v Celtic, 30 January 1965. Ogston, Bennet, Shewan, Peterson, McCormick, Smith, Fraser, Winchester, Ravn, Kerrigan, Mortensen.
415. Peter Weir. £300,000 which included Ian Scanlon in part-exchange.
416. Steve Archibald, 1980, to Tottenham. £800,000.
417. Middlesbrough.
418. 11 years.
419. 31 December 1949 v Dundee.
420. 1957.

Quiz 22

421. 1971.
422. Akranes (Iceland).
423. 95.

424. Season 1960/61. Dundee 6 Aberdeen 0 at Dens Park.
425. 1946/47, 4-0 Rangers; 1978-79, 2-1 Rangers; 1979/80, Dundee United 3-0 after 0-0 draw.
426. Raith Rovers at Kirkcaldy.
427. Raith Rovers.
428. Aberdeen 9 Queen of the South 0, 1947/48. Aberdeen 9 Raith Rovers 0, 23 August 1983.
429. Watson, Black, Hewitt.
430. Airdrie.
431. v Bayern Munich in Germany, 35,000 at the quarter-final.
432. 90,038.
433. Morton 2-1, at Cappielow.
434. Sandy Clark (Airdrie).
435. Aberdeen 6 Morton 0, 6 September 1980 at Pittodrie.
436. Mark McGhee 50; Jim Leighton 49; Willie Miller 47.
437. Hugh Hay.
438. Season 1985/86, 11 December 1985, Clydebank won 2-1. The present Clydebank was formed in 1965.
439. Manchester United, Southampton, West Ham.
440. Dundee.

Quiz 23

441. Walker McColl.
442. Harry Blackwell v Peterhead.
443. Benny Yorston.
444. Leighton, Kennedy, McMaster, Watson, McLeish, Miller, Strachan, Bell, McGhee, Jarvie, Scanlon. Subs. Garner, Cowan (Scanlon), Considine, Hewitt (Bell).
445. Dundee and St. Johnstone.
446. UEFA Cup.
447. Cup Winners Cup.
448. Akranes, European Cup Winners Cup 1983/84, 1st round, 1st leg.
449. RWD Molenbeek.
450. Dumbarton, 4 September 1899.
451. 1958.

452. 1981.
453. 14.
454. 173.
455. Peterhead.
456. Rosemount.
457. Beaten finalists.
458. Belgium at Pittodrie, November 1971.
459. Marek Dimitrov.
460. Finn Harps.

Quiz 24

461. Celtic, semi-final 0-0, Pittodrie. Celtic won 1-0 at Parkhead.
462. One. v Morton.
463. Peter Weir.
464. Manager Alex Ferguson signed a five year contract with the Dons.
465. Meadowbank Thistle, 9 November 1983. Aberdeen had previously played six games without a goal being scored against them.
466. Northern Ireland, Windsor Park, 13 December 1983.
467. Dundee at Pittodrie, 5 October 1983.
468. SK Beveran, European Cup Winners Cup, 3 November 1983.
469. Dundee, Pittodrie, 17 December 1983.
470. Dundee.
471. European Super Cup, 2nd leg v SV Hamburg at Pittodrie, 20 December 1983.
472. Simpson, McGhee.
473. Chris Harker.
474. Hugh Hay and Jimmy Wallace.
475. Bob Wishart, Graham Leggat, 1955 v England.
476. I. Jackson.
477. 7-0 v Cowdenbeath at Pittodrie.
478. Ernie McGarr.
479. Tommy Craig to Sheffield Wednesday and Jimmy Smith to Newcastle United.
480. 2nd round, Aberdeen 4 Deveronvale 2, 1960/61.

Quiz 25

481. 11 January 1947 v St. Mirren, 59th minute with Aberdeen winning 2-0.
482. Jim Hermiston.
483. 10-3, Aberdeen at Pittodrie.
484. Five. Aberdeen won 6-3.
485. v Clyde at Shawfield, 14 September 1957.
486. Elgin.
487. Five.
488. Raith Rovers.
489. Don Emery.
490. Jimmy Miller.
491. Jens Petersen.
492. 17.
493. Graham Leggat.
494. Alex Willoughby.
495. 21 visits—0 wins; 15 defeats; 6 draws.
496. 1965.
497. Stirling Albion. Dons won 6-2 away from home.
498. 19 February 1929, 3rd round, Brockville. Dons won 5-3.
499. Ernie Winchester (21).
500. Bonnyrigg Rose.

Quiz 26

Crossword 1

Down
2. Ally
3. Leighton
4. Real
5. Miller
8. Madrid
9. Hibs
10. Cat
13. Bumper
15. Pittodrie

Across
1. Ball
4. Ref
5. Milk
6. All
7. Ina
8. McLeish
11. Fab
12. Tub
14. Top

19. Beach
20. Rougvie
24. Law
26. Shock
27. AFC
29. Sit

16. Dom
17. Ian
18. Mod
21. Hit
22. Weir
23. Bell
25. Cove
28. Ferguson
30. 10
31. Coe
32. Hewitt
33. Black

Quiz 27

Crossword 2

Down

1. Sion
2. Action
3. Hibs
4. Motherwell
6. Weekend
7. Deep
13. Utd
14. Nun
15. Bayern
16. Munich
19. Love

Across

3. Home
5. Ipswich
8. Nine
9. Ice
10. Teen
11. Peter
12. Sudden
15. Bumper
17. Benny
18. Null
20. Weir
21. Dons
22. Hove

Quiz 28

1. Doug Rougvie
2. Dom Sullivan
3. Andy Harrow
4. Eric Black
5. Joe Harper

6. Drew Jarvie
7. Duncan Davidson
8. Bobby Clark
9. Willie Miller
10. Steve Archibald

Quiz 29

Graham	Ogston
Strachan	Rougvie
Miller	Gunn
Buchan	Hogg
Simpson	Davidson
Weir	Shewan
Leighton	Robb
Bell	Boel
Black	Smith
Falconer	Jarvie
Clark	

Quiz 30

501. Rangers. Seasons 1962/63/64.
502. 291.
503. FC Porto, April 1984, European Cup Winners Cup semi-final, 2nd leg.
504. None.
505. Gordon Strachan.
506. European Cup Winners Cup.
507. 1st leg, 2nd round, in Turin, 28 October 1971 Juventus won 2-0, 2nd leg at Pittodrie, 18 November 1971, 1-1.
508. 1937.
509. Doug Rougvie, 31 March 1979, Scottish League Cup final in which Rangers won 2-1.
510. Willie Miller.
511. They introduced numbers on front of their playing shirts.
512. 7 August 1984 v Dundee United at Tannadice.
513. Strachan (13); McGhee (13); Hewitt (12).
514. For 78, against 21.
515. Three.
516. 48 points.
517. Doug Rougvie v St. Mirren at Love Street. Dons lost 3-2.
518. 21.
519. 17,924.
520. Hearts 1-1, 2 April 1984.

Quiz 31

521. John Hewitt.
522. Alex McLeish v St. Johnstone—League Cup, 7 September 1983.
522. v Hearts at Tynecastle, 2/5/84, this goal also clinched Premier League title for the Dons.
524. Mark McGhee.
525. Aberdeen 1 Celtic 1. Aberdeen won 2-1 after extra time.
526. Dundee 1-0.
527. Tynecastle.
528. Eric Black, 7/1/84, v Rangers at Ibrox. Premier League game.
529. Rangers.
530. Hearts at Pittodrie 2/4/84, age 16.
531. Three: Angus, Simpson, McGhee.
532. John Hewitt (3), 1 each v Akranes home and away v IFK Gothenburg.
533. v Dundee United at Pittodrie. 18 April 1984. Aberdeen won 5-1.
534. 57 points.
535. Eight.
536. Only one, Dundee United winning 1-2, 24/9/83.
537. 322,645.
538. 16.
539. Mark McGhee.
540. £106.

Quiz 32

541. Fred Martin, George Hamilton.
542. McGhee v Dundee United and Kilmarnock. McKimmie v Kilmarnock and Celtic. Simpson v Dundee United and Dundee. Black v Dundee and Celtic.
543. Dundee, Meadowbank, St. Johnstone.
544. Manchester United and Cologne.
545. v St Johnstone, 30 April 1984.
546. Mark McGhee.

547. Mark McGhee, European Cup Winners Cup quarter-final 2nd leg at Pittodrie, 21 March 1984, against Upjest Dozsa.

548. Referee limped off seven minutes from half-time and a linesman took over and substitute linesman was called in.

549. Gordon Strachan (40 minutes with a penalty v Dundee at Pittodrie).

550. Four.

551. Stewart Kennedy, Joe Harper.

552. No.

553. Angus, Cooper v Clyde 4th Round, 18 February 1984.

554. Mark McGhee, 10 times.

555. John Hewitt.

556. McGhee (5), Strachan (3), Simpson (1), Weir (1).

557. There were no penalties against Aberdeen in Premier League games season 1983/84.

558. Hearts at Tynecastle.

559. Celtic at Parkhead 1-0, 31/3/84.

560. Dundee United.

Quiz 33

561. Graham Leggat.

562. (1) 1 (2), 2 (3) 5.

563. McMaster v Dundee United at Pittodrie 24 September 1983. Strachan v Celtic at Pittodrie 22 October 1983.

564. Eric Black v Raith Rovers, League Cup, 24 August 1983. Billy Stark v St. Mirren, Premier League, 12 May 1984.

565. 12 May 1984 v St. Mirren at Love Street.

566. Raith Rovers at Pittodrie 24 August 1983.

567. Dundee United at Pittodrie 24/9/83 1-2. Hibs at Easter Road 15/10/83 2-1. Celtic at Parkhead 31/3/84 1-0. St. Mirren at Love Street 12/5/84 3-2.

568. St. Mirren in last game of season at Love Street 3-2.

569. St. Johnstone (twice) 3/9/83, Pittodrie 5-0. 5/11/83 Muirton 0-

5. Dundee 31/12/83 Pittodrie 5-2. Dundee United 18/4/84 Pittodrie 5-1.

570. Mark McGhee, 2nd minute.
571. Jim Leighton, Alex McLeish, Willie Miller, Gordon Strachan.
572. 18.
573. Dundee United, Airdrie, Raith Rovers.
574. Doug Rougvie.
575. Martin Buchan.
576. West Germany.
577. Dundee at Pittodrie, 11 August 1984.
578. Billy Stark v Dundee at Pittodrie, 11 August 1984.
579. Brian Grant.
580. Arthur Graham.

Quiz 34

581. Aberdeen 2 Queens Park 1. 20 January 1905.
582. St. Mirren at Love Street 18 August 1984. Dons won 2-0.
583. Coach for Scotland.
584. Skol League Cup 2nd round as a sub v Airdrie, 22 August 1984.
585. George Taylor.
586. 1,500 shares. Cost per share £1.
587. 14 April 1903.
588. John Clark.
589. Peter Simpson.
590. Willie McAuly.
591. Willie McAuly.
592. Eric Black v Morton at Cappielow, Saturday 8 September 1984.
593. Hearts at Tynecastle, 12 August 1978.
594. Yes. Season 1981/82 v Rangers at Pittodrie, Dons won 4-0.
595. McAuly 12 goals.
596. John Clark.

597. Barret, McGregor, Willox, Sangster, H. Low, R. Ritchie, C. Mackie, Strang, R. McKay, W. McAuly, Johnstone.
598. Lose. Alloa won 2-1 in 1st round.
599. Aberdeenshire Cup beating Bon Accord 3-2 at home.
600. Jimmy Delaney.

Quiz 35

601. Harry Melrose.
602. Arthur Graham, Willie Miller, Ian Purdie.
603. Goalkeeper, Bobby Clark.
604. 0-6 v Clydebank, last game of season 3 May 1986.
605. Jim Hamilton going to East Fife with Bertie Miller coming to Pittodrie.
606. Ian MacFarlane.
607. Ian Taylor.
608. November 1969, £20,000.
609. Queens Park, St. Johnstone, Dunfermline, Rangers, Falkirk.
610. Matt Armstrong.
611. v Celtic at Parkhead 6 October 1984.
612. Tommy Craig, from Aberdeen to Sheffield Wednesday in 1969.
613. Willie Miller, Eric Black.
614. Ian Angus.
615. Johnstone after a 0-0 draw at Pittodrie—Johnstone won 2-1 on their own ground.
616. Charlie O'Hagan.
617. Goalkeeper Bobby Clark.
618. Alloa Athletic.
619. Aberdeen have scored 283 goals against St. Mirren.
620. Celtic 281, Aberdeen 211; Hearts 225, Aberdeen 215; Rangers 264, Aberdeen 202; Third Lanark 132, Aberdeen 127; Bo'ness 1 Aberdeen 0.

Quiz 36

621. Billy Little, 16 goals.
622. Aberdeen 11 SV Hamburg 2.

Picture Quiz 24
Signed from Banks O' Dee in 1952–and was transferred to Fulham in August 1958?

623. Kenneth Thomson.
624. Dons keeper Bobby Clark came on as a sub for the injured Jim Forrest and played in an outfield position.
625. Opened Saturday 30 September 1972 at 57 Nelson Street, Aberdeen.
626. Willie Callaghan.
627. George Kinnell.
628. Round 1, 1910, Aberdeen won 3-0.
629. Season 1909/10, at Pittodrie Aberdeen 3 Bo'ness 0.
630. Billy McNeill, 8 July 1977 just a month after he had taken over at Pittodrie.
631. Season 1946/47.
632. Clyde. Scottish Cup season 1961/62.
633. Billy McNeill, June 1977 to May 1978.
634. 1903-1924 Jimmy Phillip. 1924-1937 Paddy Travers. 1938-June 1955 Dave Halliday. 1955-November 1959 Dave Shaw. November 1959-March 1965 Tommy Pearson. March 1967-1971 Eddie Turnbull. August 1971-October 1975 Jimmy Bonthrone. November 1975-May 1977 Ally McLeod. June 1977-May 1978, Billy McNeill. June 1978 Alex Ferguson.
635. Arbroath FC.
636. Season 1972/73.
637. Season 1934/35, 2-1 at Parkhead.
638. Season 1946/47.
639. 314, stretching from October 1963 to May 1969.
640. Paddy Moore, 28 goals.

Quiz 37

641. Aberdeen's first home Scottish Cup tie v Queens Park. Aberdeen won 2-1.
642. Jimmy Mitchell.
643. George Murray.
644. 23 March 1968 v Motherwell at Fir Park. Dons won 3-0.
645. S. Murray, Harper, Hermiston, Willoughby.
646. 10.
647. KRR Reykjavik, 2nd leg Cup Winners Cup 1967/68.
648. Two. 1 v Slavia Sofia 1968/69. 1 v Finn Harps 1973/74.

649. Season 1954/55.
650. 1935/36.
651. Jimmy Smith.
652. Season 1957/58 (76 goals).
653. Willie Miller (51).
654. Six.
655. Drew Jarvie v RWD Molenbeek. UEFA Cup 1st round.
656. Munro (3), Smith (2), Storrie (2), McMillan, Taylor, Petersen. v KRR Reykjavik, season 1967/68, European Cup Winners Cup.
657. Honved at Pittodrie season 1970/71. Cup Winners Cup.
658. Fraserburgh.
659. Billy Stark, Willie Falconer, Steve Gray all v Akranes. Frank McDougall v Servette.
660. Four.

Quiz 38

661. Ismaili. 2-2.
662. 9 December 1967. Came on as a sub v Kilmarnock.
663. Joseph Montgomery Harper.
664. 32 points. Season 1975/76.
665. Graham Leggat. Billy Little scored the Dons other goal.
666. Juventus at Pittodrie, 17 November 1971.
667. July 1969.
668. Clyde 14 September 1957, League Cup. Aberdeen lost 4-2.
669. v Rangers at Pittodrie, 19 January 1985. Aberdeen won 5-1.
670. v Falkirk, February 1950.
671. Billy Stark.
672. Andy Watson.
673. £125,000.
674. 14.
675. 3rd—53 points.
676. Three.
677. Mark McGhee v Memphis at Pittodrie.
678. Jim Whyte.
679. v Celtic, 28 March 1981.
680. Willie Cooper.

Quiz 39

681. Anderson.
682. Colman.
683. Tom Noble.
684. Cail (8), Walker (8).
685. Season 1906/07.
686. Walker McCall.
687. Fulham, October 1959.
688. Robert Russell, October 1959.
689. Once, round 5, season 1954/55. Dons won 6-0.
690. Twice. Season 1919/20 Dons won 1-0 away? Dons won 2-0 away.
691. Twice. Round 1, 1937/38, Dons won 6-1 away and won 5-0 home.
692. Season 1963/64, draw 1-1 at Pittodrie, Dons won replay 2-1 after extra time.
693. Raith Rovers at Starks Park, 4th Round, Dons won 1-2, 16 February 1985.
694. Ian Scanlon, Aberdeen won 4-1. Other Dons scorer Andy Watson.
695. 21 August 1980 v Fraserburgh in a reserve match played at Fraserburgh.
696. Steve Murray.
697. Viktor Pepovic.
698. Andy Harrow.
699. Celtic at Parkhead, 28 March 1981, 1-1.
700. Paddy Wilson.

Quiz 40

701. Tommy Lowrie.
702. Season 1980/81.
703. 11.
704. 18.
705. Benny Yorston (24) 1928-31.
706. Jacky Connon (14).

707. Dod Brewster.
708. Benny Yorston, (10) 1928/29.
709. Bobby Cummings v Clyde, 1961/62. Norman Davidson v Brechin, 1959/60. W. D. Nicol v Forfar 1910/11.
710. Joe O'Neil.
711. Harry Yorston.
712. Steve Archibald v Airdrie, 1979/80.
713. Hearts.
714. Hearts at Pittodrie, 9 February 1985.
715. Alex McLeish, Mark McGhee.
716. Sion (Switzerland) 2,400, preliminary round, European Cup Winners Cup, 1 September 1982.
717. 15 games, season 1975/76.
718. 50 goals, season 1975/76.
719. 7th, season 1975/76.
720. Season 1979/80.

Quiz 41

721. T. Murray, season 1907/08.
722. Harry Yorston.
723. v Morton, 6 December 1980, away.
724. v Dundee United, home, season 1977/78.
725. 11. Aberdeen registered their first win 11 October 1952, winning 4-3 v Third Lanark.
726. Greenock.
727. Stonehaven.
728. Willie Falconer, John Hewitt, Stewart McKimmie.
729. Doug Bell, Steve Cowan.
730. Dave Main.
731. 6th—36 points.
732. Season 1936/37, Scottish Cup final v Celtic, Hampden, crowd 144,550.
733. Sandy Clark.
734. Eric Black (2), Ian Angus (1).
735. Harper 3 v Celtic Vigo. 1 v Juventus. Forrest (1) v Celtic Vigo.
736. v KRR Reykjavik, Cup Winners Cup, season 1967/68, Munro, Smith, Storrie, McMillan, Taylor, Petersen, M. Buchan.

737. Fairs Cup.
738. Doug Considine.
739. A. Rankin.
740. 5th.

Quiz 42

741. Andy Watson.
742. Ally McLeod.
743. Eric Black.
744. Eddie Fallon, Paddy Moore, Charlie O'Hagan.
745. Paddy Moore, Joe O'Reilly.
746. Bobby Clark, Ernie McGarr.
747. Seven.
748. Five.
749. Fred Martin, Reg Morrison.
750. Dumbarton beat them 2-1 in the 2nd round.
751. 7th, 43 points.
752. 1934.
753. 1983.
754. Eric Black, John Hewitt.
755. St. Clair.
756. Season 1977/78, Aberdeen won 2 games, 1-0 and drew 0-0 in remaining two games.
757. Ian Polworth.
758. Three times, 3 May 1980, Easter Road; 14 May 1983, Pittodrie; 23 March 1985, Easter Road.
759. 5-0 at Pittodrie, 8 October 1983.
760. Twice, 1 May 1982, 5-0 at Dens Park. 31 December 1983, 5-2 at Pittodrie.

Quiz 43

761. Season 1980/81, 6 September 1980.
762. Joe Harper at Pittodrie, season 1978-79.
763. St Johnstone.

764. 3 Premier League Championships, 4 Scottish Cups, European Cup Winners Cup, European Super Cup, Skol League Cup, Drybrough Cup (1 each).
765. 22.
766. Rangers failed to register a win losing 3, drawing 1.
767. v Rangers at Ibrox 6 April 1985.
768. Rangers Boys Club and Banks O Dee A.
769. Season 1972/73, 20 February 1973.
770. Frank Dunlop.
771. Jim Hermiston and Dave Robb.
772. Charlie Cooke.
773. Dundee 0 Aberdeen 5, 1st round. Dundee United 0 Aberdeen 1, semi-final. Both at Dens Park.
774. Chris Harker, Tommy Pearson.
775. Steve Murray.
776. 1917/18, 1918/19.
777. Neale Cooper.
778. Newcastle United won 4-0.
779. 1952, Aberdeen won 3-2 after a 2-2 draw.
780. Season 1984/85, semi-final replay, Dundee United 2 Aberdeen 1.

Quiz 44

781. Season 1962/63. 1st round.
782. Season 1936/37. 1950/51.
783. George Hamilton v Belgium 1951.
784. Billy Stark (4).
785. 10,000 all ticket 4th round v Raith Rovers at Starks Park.
786. Tommy McQueen.
787. Ian Angus.
788. Aberdeen won all four games.
789. Jim Tolmie.
790. 1929. League game v Rangers.
791. 13 March 1954. Scottish Cup quarter-final v Hearts.
792. Season 1910/11. 3rd round tie.
793. Bozo Bakota of Sturm Graz.
794. Neil Simpson. Jim Leighton.

795. Season 1984/85. 27 April 1985. By drawing with Celtic 1-1.
796. Willie Miller v Celtic at Pittodrie 27 April 1985.
797. Jimmy Jackson.
798. Liverpool. Game ended 1-1.
799. Semi-final replay v Dundee United, season 1984/85.
800. Archie Glen v Clyde 1-0, 9 April 1955.

Quiz 45

801. Bob Fraser
802. Aberdeen lost 4-0 to Celtic.
803. Blackwell and Maclachlan. 38 appearances each.
804. v St. Mirren at Pittodrie 2 March 1985. v Hearts at Tynecastle 4 May 1985.
805. Reserve League Cup.
806. Eric Black v Hibs 23 March 1985. McDougall v Rangers 19 January 1985. McDougall v Hearts 4 May 1985.
807. Lost both games 4-1 v Dundee United 29 August 1981. 3-1 v Celtic 5 September 1981.
808. 8-0. Dons won 5-0 at home and 3-0 away.
809. McLeish, McGhee, Stark, Cooper.
810. 11.
811. 6.
812. Mark McGhee, 23 August 1980.
813. 4-0 v Liverpool. European Cup 2nd round, 2nd leg (away), 5 November 1980.
814. 6. UEFA Cup Season 1971/72. Away from home to Borussia Moenchengladbach.
815. Tony Fitzpatrick.
816. Premier League 28 March 1981 v Celtic at Parkhead.
817. Regina.
818. Twice. 5 January 1985 v Hibs at Pittodrie. 11 May 1985 v Morton at Cappielow.
819. Dundee.
820. Leighton (34), McKimmie (34), Miller (34), McQueen (33) plus twice as substitute.

Quiz 46

821. Tommy McQueen (3).
822. Dundee United 1-0, 22 December 1984.
823. Morton at Cappielow. 11 May 1985. Last game of season, 1,500.
824. St. Mirren. Aberdeen won 2-1 at Hampden, 2 August 1980.
825. Kenny Thomson.
826. (1st) Frank McDougall, (24). Billy Stark (3rd) (22).
827. 17.
828. White shirts and stockings, black shorts.
829. Derek Hamilton.
830. Morton 1-0 at Cappielow.
831. Andy Graham.
832. Neil Connell.
833. Iceland, 29 May 1985. Scotland won 1-0.
834. Jimmy Bonthrone.
835. Partick Thistle away from home, Dons won 2-1.
836. Pre-season West German tour v BW Berlin, 3 August 1984, Dons lost 1-0.
837. Leicester City centenary match.
838. John McGachie.
839. Dundee United, 29 September 1983.
840. Cappielow was frozen.

Quiz 47

841. Doug Bell, Tommy McIntyre, Steve Cowan.
842. Bob Fraser.
843. Frank McDougall.
844. v Rangers at Ibrox, 17 November 1984.
845. Brian Irvine.
846. Switzerland.
847. Sion. Game ended in a goal-less draw.
848. Steve Cowan.
849. v Hibs at Pittodrie, 10 August 1985.
850. Hibs. League game at Pittodrie, 10 August 1985.

851. 85 (53 as substitute).
852. 28 August 1985 v St. Johnstone. Muirton Park. Skol League Cup, 3rd round.
853. Leighton, McLeish, Miller, Bett.
854. Akranes in European Cup, 1st round, 1st leg away from home, 18 September 1985.
855. Huddersfield Town. The game ended in a 2-2 draw.
856. Raith Rovers.
857. European Cup, 2 October 1985 at Pittodrie, 1st round, 2nd leg v Akranes.
858. Ipswich Town. UEFA Cup at Pittodrie, 16 September 1981.
859. Eddie Thomson.
860. Paul Wright.

Quiz 48

861. Doug Bell
862. v Hibs at Pittodrie, 10 August 1985.
863. £45,000.
864. Alex McLeish.
865. v Akranes. European Cup 1st round, 1st leg, away from home. 18 September 1985.
866. 9 October 1985, Skol Cup semi-final, 2nd leg, v Dundee United.
867. v Hibs at Easter Road, 12 October 1985.
868. Alex McLeish.
869. Akranes European Cup at Pittodrie, 2 October 1985.
870. Jack Beattie.
871. Scandinavia.
872. Montrose 13-0.
873. Queens Park.
874. Eastercraigs.
875. Stan Williams.
876. £115,000-£125,000.
877. 215.
878. Barnsley and Grimsby Town.
879. Martin Buchan.
880. v Servette, 23 October 1985, European Cup, 2nd round, 1st leg.

Picture Quiz 25
Although born in India–this former Aberdeen FC player has represented Scotland at youth
and Under 21 level–now with Aston Villa?

Quiz 49

881. Black (2), Stark (1).
882. None.
883. Skol League Cup final, 27 October 1985.
884. Tommy Walker.
885. Frank McDougall. Premier League game at Pittodrie.
886. Skol League Cup. Sunday 27 October 1985.
887. George Hamilton, 2 January 1947, at Parkhead. Dons won 5-1. Frank McDougall, 2 November 1985, at Pittodrie. Dons won 4-1.
888. Angus, Weir, J. Miller.
889. Neil Simpson.
890. v Dundee United at Tannadice. Premier League game 21 December 1985.
891. Scoring in eight successive League games. A feat only achieved previously by Hibs Ally McLeod, season 1977/78.
892. East Fife (1903).
893. Aberdeen Juniors.
894. Aberdeen and Montrose had never met in a Scottish Cup tie prior to their meeting in 1985/86.
895. Jocky Scott, 10 January 1976 at Pittodrie, Dons won 5-3. Graham scored the other two goals.
896. St. Johnstone scored no goals v Dons in Premier League games in that season. Dons won all four games.
897. Jim Rust.
898. Ian Fleming (approximately £15,000).
899. Charles Elvin.
900. Tennents Sixes Trophy.

Quiz 50

901. Five. Eddie Turnbull, Jimmy Bonthrone, Ally McLeod, Billy McNeill, Alex Ferguson.
902. Ian Fleming, 1 goal, 5 November 1977 at Tannadice. Ian Fleming, 1 goal, 2 January 1978 at Pittodrie. Other two games ended in 0-0 draw.

903. £1.50.
904. 3-2 Aberdeen.
905. 1955/56 Graham Leggat (29). 1950/51 George Hamilton (29).
906. Paddy Moore.
907. Matt Armstrong, Billy Strauss.
908. Five.
909. Benny Yorston, 46 goals, season 1929/30.
910. IFK Gothenburg, 5 March 1986, European Cup quarter-final, 1st leg, at Pittodrie.
911. Willie Miller.
912. Sam Cail and Joe Walker.
913. St. Mirren 1959.
914. Martin, Hamilton.
915. Only once.
916. Eric Black. Dons won 4-1. Bett was the Dons other scorer.
917. Andy Cowie.
918. 14 November 1925, Dundee United 2 Aberdeen 0.
919. None.
920. Hamilton Accies.

Quiz 51

921. False. Joe Harper played for Everton.
922. False.
923. False. He was Aberdeen's third manager. Jimmy Phillips was the first.
924. True.
925. False. 1971. 1980.
926. True.
927. True.
928. False. Ferguson took over in June 1978.
929. False.
930. True.
931. False. Dunfermline United.
932. False. Martin Buchan won in season 1970/71.
933. True.

934. True.
935. True.
936. True.
937. False. He had trials with Aston Villa.
938. False. Albion Rovers won 2-1 on 6 March 1920.
939. True.
940. True.

Quiz 52

941. Ally McLeod, season 1976/77.
942. Hearts. 1st leg 3-3, 2nd leg 1-0.
943. 1st.
944. Rangers.
945. Home win two points, home draw one point, away win 3 points, away draw 2 points.
946. Archie Baird.
947. Reggie Morrison.
948. St. Johnstone.
949. Three.
950. Davie Shaw.
951. North East Cup, aggregate 7-6. Mitchell Trophy aggregate 6-5.
952. Davie Shaw.
953. Archie Baird.
954. Scotland v Wales. 1900.
955. 1928.
956. Famous Five.
957. Jimmy Jackson from Motherwell, summer of 1923.
958. One shilling (5p).
959. Falkirk.
960. Rangers.

Quiz 53

961. Ayr United.
962. Matt Armstrong.

963. Ian Scanlon from Notts County. Gordon Strachan from Dundee. Steve Archibald from Clyde. Steve Ritchie from Hereford. Doug Considine from Huntly.
964. Peter Simpson (former Victoria United trainer).
965. Willie McAuly v Stenhousemuir. Score 1-1.
966. Rob MacFarlane.
967. Falkirk, 20 August 1904. Falkirk won 2-1.
968. St. Ternan (Banchory).
969. Patrick Boyle and Tom Strang.
970. Tom Murray.
971. Motherwell. 11 November 1916, winning 2-1.
972. Alex Mutch.
973. Robert Blackburn.
974. Jock Hume.
975. Season 1916/17.
976. Dave Main, for then a record four seasons in a row.
977. Scottish Cup 4th round v Arbroath at Gayfield 15 February 1986. Dons won 1-0.
978. Arbroath won 2-1 at Gayfield, season 1931/32.
979. Season 1969/70.
980. 9th (32 points).

Quiz 54

981. "Cody"
982. True, going down in first round to East Fife 1-0 after a 0-0 draw.
983. False. 1959.
984. Bobby Bruce—23 goals.
985. True. They were drawn away from home in all their games.
986. Johnstone (1947).
987. False. He was manager of Forfar Athletic.
988. Season 1962/63, first round.
989. 36—season 1904/05 Division 2. 36—season 1916/17 Division 1.

990. 24—season 1916/17.
991. 11 times—seasons 1912/13, 1920/21, 1936/37, 1947/48, 1950/51, 1951/52, 1952/53, 1953/54, 1957/58, 1960/61, 1962/63.
992. Sunnybank.
993. Ian Gibson to Kilmarnock for £17,500.
994. From July 1952 to March 1953.
995. Partick Thistle, East Fife, Dundee, Stirling Albion, Queen of the South.
996. On three occasions, 1926/27, 1937/38, 1964/65.
997. False—the game was in Egypt.
998. False. Andy Watson went to Leeds United from Aberdeen, then from Leeds to Hearts.
999. £2.80.
1000 Jimmy Bonthrone.
1001 1964/65, going out to East Fife 1-0 after a 0-0 draw. 1973/74, going out in 3rd round 2-0 to Dundee.

Picture Quiz Answers

1. Arthur Graham
2. Archie Glen
3. Derek McKay
4. Davie Shaw
5. Joe Harper
6. Alley McLeod
7. Ally Shewan
8. 1982
9. Dave Halliday
10. Bobby Calder
11. Drew Jarvie
12. Willie Young
13. Jimmy Mitchell
14. Zoltan Varga
15. Don Emery
16. Martin Buchan
17. Billy McNeill
18. 1947
19. George Hamilton and Harry Yorston
20. Doug Rougvie
21. Jimmy Bonthrone
22. Jim Hermiston
23. John Ogston
24. Graham Leggat
25. Neale Cooper

THE DONS' QUIZ BOOK

Diary: Season 1985/86

"A year in the life of the Dons" 1985/86

Pre-Season: Dons sign Brian Irvine from Falkirk for a fee in the region of £80,000.Neale Cooper signs a one-year contract with the Dons. Steve Cowan signs for Hibs for a fee in the region of £45,000. Cowan made 85 first-team appearances for the Dons—53 as a sub in his six years at Pittodrie.

Saturday 10 August 1985	**Premier League**
Aberdeen 3 Hibs 0	**Crowd 15,000**

The first goal came in the 68th minute. Peter Weir chipped a corner from the left to Jim Bett stationed just outside the box. **Bett** controlled the ball and blasted it into the Hibs top left-hand corner.

Goal number two came in the 79th minute and started with a Billy Stark cross which **Frank McDougall** forced in with his head despite the keeper's valiant attempt to stop the ball from squirming over the line.

Number three was beautifully created and taken. A Jim Bett cross from the left, a touch in from the right by Neil Simpson and a diving header from **Frank McDougall.**

Aberdeen:
Leighton, McKimmie, McQueen, Stark, McLeish, Miller, Black, Simpson, McDougall, Bett, Weir. Sub: Hewitt for Black.

Saturday 17 August 1985	**Premier League**
Dundee United 1 Aberdeen 1	**Crowd 15,000**

After weathering United's aggressive opening, Aberdeen replied in typical fashion. Billy Stark evaded a lunging Dodds tackle and played a great pass to **Stewart McKimmie** who hit a well judged dipping shot from 22-yards, which beat the United keeper all the way—putting the Dons one up in the 36th minute.

Paul Sturrock equalised for United in the 42nd minute.

Aberdeen:

Gunn, McKimmie, Cooper, Stark, McLeish, Miller, Black, Simpson, McDougall, Bett, Weir. Sub: Hewitt for Black.

Doug Bell signs for Rangers. Bell made 215 first-team appearances for Aberdeen since joining them in 1979.

Wednesday 21 August 1985   **Skol Cup 2nd round**
Aberdeen 5 Ayr United 0   **Crowd 12,000**

Following a corner on the left in the third minute Bett sent in a 25-yard drive which the Ayr keeper could only parry and **Stark** followed up and put the ball in the back of the net.

Goal number two came in the 39th minute following a melee in the Ayr goal area which resulted in a penalty which **McQueen** tucked into the left hand corner of the Ayr net.

There was a touch of inevitability about Aberdeen's third goal in 55 minutes. A cross from Miller on the right was met by **Stark**, and although the Ayr keeper got his hands to the header, the ball continued into the roof of the net.

McDougall redeemed himself for an earlier miss when he claimed the fourth goal in 84 minutes, sending the ball into the net from the edge of the six yard box.

It was **McDougall** again two minutes later when his snap header from a Bett cross from the right beat the Ayr keeper at the near post.

Aberdeen:

Gunn, McKimmie, McQueen, Stark, McLeish, Miller, Hewitt, Simpson, McDougall, Bett, Weir. Subs: Cooper for McKimmie, Black for Simpson.

Saturday 24 August 1985   **Premier League**
Aberdeen 1 Motherwell 1   **Crowd 14,000**

Motherwell went into this game knowing it was 19 years ago that they last won a League game at Pittodrie. Aberdeen opened the scoring in the 19th minute, Bett turned the ball into the tracks of **McKimmie** who fired a raging 25-yard drive outwith the reach of the Motherwell keeper.

Motherwell equalised in the 33rd minute with a Blair goal.

Aberdeen:
Gunn, McKimmie, McQueen, Stark, McLeish, Miller, Hewitt, Simpson, McDougall, Bett, Weir. Subs: Cooper for McQueen, Black for McDougall.

Wednesday 28 August 1985   Skol League Cup 3rd round
St. Johnstone 0 Aberdeen 2   Crowd 5,000

Aberdeen took the lead in the 27th minute. McDougall took a long forward pass from McKimmie, deceived the opposition with a clever inward turn before sending away **Hewitt** who ran on to fire a left-foot shot into the roof of the net from just inside the box.

In the 86th minute **McDougall** guided a header well clear of the Saints keeper from a Miller free kick on the right to put the Dons two up.

Steve Gray made his first-team debut in competitive football for the Dons.

Aberdeen:
Gunn, McKimmie, McQueen, Gray, McLeish, Miller, Hewitt, Simpson, McDougall, Bett, Weir. Sub: Stark for McQueen.

Saturday 31 August 1985   Premier League
Dundee 1 Aberdeen 3   Crowd 7,592

Following an even first half, it didn't take Aberdeen long to raise their game and secure the points. Bett fired a powerful cut-back straight into **Neil Simpson's** path.

Dons second came after Shannon had been booked for a lunge at McKimmie, from the resulting free-kick Miller exposed the Dundee defence and **Billy Stark** rose unchallenged to head home with great power.

Ten minutes from the end **Stark** again appeared at the back post, this time to head home a cross from Simpson.

In the last minute, Dundee achieved something which never looked likely, a goal! scored by on loan striker Russell Black. As a note of interest Dundee last beat Aberdeen at Dens Park on 31 August 1975.

Aberdeen:
Leighton, McKimmie, Mitchell, Stark, McLeish, Miller, Black,

Simpson, McDougall, Bett, Weir. Subs: McIntyre for McDougall, Hewitt for Weir.

Wednesday 4 September 1985   **Skol Cup quarter-final**
Aberdeen 1 Hearts 0   **Crowd 14,000**

An Aberdeen goal was not unexpected in the 24th minute. It was a simple affair, a McKimmie cross from the right seemed to threaten little danger but Smith and McDonald got themselves in a tangle and **Black** was able to turn the ball into the net.

Aberdeen:
Leighton, McKimmie, Mitchell, Stark, McLeish, Miller, Black, Simpson, McDougall, Bett, Weir.

Saturday 7 September 1985   **Premier League**
Aberdeen 3 Hearts 0   **Crowd 14,000**

It was a Hewitt corner which broke the deadlock in the 32nd minute. Mitchell appeared on the right to return Hewitt's kick from the left and with the Heart's defence in their first mix-up of the game **Billy Stark** stooped to head the ball over the line.

With 72 minutes gone Aberdeen called in teenager **Paul Wright** for his Premier League debut in place of Stark. And the youngster needed only three minutes to find the net. The 18-year-old cut in from the left and had the Hearts keeper grasping the air with a right-foot drive into the top left-hand corner.

In the dying minutes of the game **Eric Black** made it three with a brilliant header from a Hewitt cross.

Aberdeen:
Leighton, McKimmie, Mitchell, Stark, McLeish, Miller, Black, Simpson, McDougall, Bett, Hewitt. Subs: Cooper for McDougall, Wright for Stark.

Saturday 14 September 1985   **Premier League**
Celtic 2 Aberdeen 1   **Crowd 39,450**

Celtic went into the lead in the 32nd minute via a McClair goal, and there the score stood until five minutes from the end, **McDougall** took full advantage of a mix-up in the Celtic defence to lash the ball over the line from only a couple of yards. McGrain had chested a Miller shot off the line. But with only two minutes left McClair headed in from a Provan corner.

Following this game Aberdeen were in third place in the

League three points behind leaders Rangers.

Aberdeen:
Leighton, McKimmie, Mitchell, Stark, McLeish, Miller, Black, Simpson, McDougall, Bett, Hewitt. Subs: Weir for Hewitt, Cooper for Stark.

Wednesday 18 September   **European Cup, 1st round, 1st leg**
Akranes 1 Aberdeen 3   **Crowd 7,000**

The Dons got a shock when Akranes took the lead in the 36th minute from a spot kick in which Ingolfsson sent Leighton the wrong way.

Black struck the post with a fierce drive from a Hewitt lay-off then the vital goal came when he rose to meet a Bett cross and find the corner of the net with a high-leaping header in the 56th minute.

In the 62nd minute the Dons took the lead—a McQueen cross from the left was touched on by Black to Bett, and **Hewitt** nipped in to finish the move with a close-range shot.

Two minutes later the Dons increased their lead when **Stark** netted a header after a build-up on the right between Gray and Bett.

Aberdeen:
Leighton, McKimmie, McQueen, Stark, McLeish, Miller, Black, Cooper, Hewitt, Bett, Gray.
Subs: Mitchell for Stark, Wright for Black.

Saturday 21 September 1985   **Premier League**
Aberdeen 1 St. Mirren 1   **Crowd 13,000**

Aberdeen opened the scoring in the 46th minute with a well-taken spot-kick by **Tommy McQueen.** Another penalty award this time in St. Mirren's favour gave them a share of the points in the 62nd minute.

Aberdeen:
Leighton, McKimmie, McQueen, Stark, McLeish, Miller, Black, Cooper, Hewitt, Bett, Gray.
Subs: McDougall for McQueen, Porteous for Hewitt.

Wednesday 25 September 1985   Skol Cup semi-final, 1st leg
Dundee United 0 Aberdeen 1   Crowd 12,837

In the only goal in the game which came in the 63rd minute.
Miller moved upfield before sending Hewitt away on the left.
When Hewitt crossed **Black** rose in the goalmouth to head into
the net.

Aberdeen:

Leighton, McKimmie, Mitchell, Stark, McLeish, Miller, Black,
Simpson, McDougall, Cooper, Hewitt.
Subs: Gray for Simpson, Falconer for McDougall.

Saturday 28 September 1985   Premier League
Rangers 0 Aberdeen 3   Crowd 37,599

Aberdeen took the lead in the 30th minute when they scored
from a free kick awarded when Burns was sent off after a foul on
Hewitt.

Hewitt took the kick, and **McLeish** beat the Ibrox heads to
crash the ball past the Rangers keeper.

Eight minutes later, **Billy Stark** hit Rangers with a second
goal—a McDougall header came off the bar, making it easy for
Stark to tuck it away.

Hewitt hit a third with a thoughtful lob over the Rangers
keeper in the 79th minute.

Aberdeen:

Leighton, McKimmie, Mitchell, Stark, McLeish, Miller, Black,
Simpson, McDougall, Cooper Hewitt.

Wednesday 2 October 1985 European Cup, 1st round, 2nd leg
Aberdeen 4 Akranes 1 (aggregate 7-2)   Crowd 14,500

Aberdeen took the early lead they were looking for with a goal in
five minutes. A Gray cross from the right was dropped by the
Akranes keeper and the ball broke clear to **Simpson**, whose try
from the edge of the box went into the net off the underside of
the crossbar.

The Icelanders produced a surprise equaliser in 32 minutes
after Leighton had failed to collect the ball as he dived off his line.
Johannesson turned the ball into the net.

In the 63rd minute the Dons went ahead when **Hewitt** volleyed the ball into the net after a right wing move involving Gray and McKimmie.

Aberdeen increased their lead in 65 minutes when **Gray** met an Angus cross at the near post and headed the ball into the net.

Two minutes later **Falconer** joined the scoring list when he netted from 10 yards after a Simpson shot had been blocked.

Aberdeen:

Leighton, McKimmie, Mitchell, Gray, McLeish, Miller, Black, Simpson, Wright, Cooper, Hewitt.

Subs: Angus for Mitchell, Falconer for Wright.

Saturday 5 October 1985   **Premier League**
Aberdeen 3 Clydebank 1   **Crowd 11,500**

The Dons opening goal came with only a minute played. An outswinging free from Hewitt on the left was touched away by the keeper but only onto **Black's** head, from where it sped into the net.

Conroy equalised for the visitors in the 7th minute. However the Dons went one up in the 9th minute. Hewitt from his beat on the left cut back to diddle a Clydebank player and right footed a low cross which **McDougall** met first-time for a glorious goal.

The Dons made it 3-1 in the 86th minute when **McKimmie** burst onto a loose ball which he put into the back of the net.

Aberdeen:

Leighton, McKimmie, Mitchell, Stark, McLeish, Miller, Black, Simpson, McDougall, Cooper, Hewitt.

Subs: Angus for Stark, Falconer for Black.

Wednesday 9 October 1985   **Skol Cup semi-final, 2nd leg**
Aberdeen 1 Dundee United 0   **Crowd 20,000**

In the 68th minute Pittodrie was a bedlam of noise when McDougall finally gave Aberdeen their overdue lead. It all started with a Leighton punch-out that was gathered by Angus, who sent Hewitt away on the left. The winger's low cross was clinically first-timed by **McDougall** past the helpless United keeper.

Aberdeen:
Leighton, McKimmie, Mitchell, Stark, McLeish, Miller, Angus, Simpson, McDougall, Cooper, Hewitt.
Sub: Gray for Stark.

Saturday 12 October 1985   **Premier League**
Hibs 1 Aberdeen 1   **Crowd 12,000**

Ex-Don Steve Cowan put Hibs in the lead in the 25th minute with a well-taken header.

In the 82nd minute **Gray** gathered a Neale Cooper chip and squeezed the ball under the keeper from a tight angle to make the final score 1-1.

Aberdeen:
Leighton, McKimmie, Mitchell, Stark, McLeish, Miller, Angus, Simpson, McDougall, Cooper, Hewitt.
Subs: Gray for Mitchell, Wright for Simpson.
Footnote: Alex McLeish made his 400th first-team appearance for Aberdeen. Steve Gray scored his first Premier League goal for the Dons.

Saturday 19 October 1985   **Premier League**
Aberdeen 3 Dundee United 2   **Crowd 15,800**

The home side were given a shock in the early minutes when United struck with a superb goal from Sturrock.

But Aberdeen were quickly back in business with a **Hewitt** volley from 10 yards, following a perfect cross from the right by Gray.

The Dons went ahead in the 17th minute. Simpson sent over a cross from the left and **McDougall** beat Thomson with a superb header from six yards.

The Dons were in action again in the 24th minute. **Hewitt** caught the ball on the bye-line, pulled it inside the six-yard box, evading tackles from all angles—and crashed home a close-range shot.

United pulled one back soon after the restart, when Redford got on the end of a waist-high cross from McGinness to net with a diving header.

Aberdeen:
Leighton, Mitchell, McKimmie, Stark, McLeish, Miller, Gray, Simpson, McDougall, Cooper, Hewitt.
Subs: Black for Gray, McIntyre for Simpson.

Wednesday 23 October 1985European Cup, 2nd round, 1st leg
Servette 0 Aberdeen 0   **Crowd 8,000**

This was the 10th shut-out the Dons have produced in 33 European games away from home.

The Geneva game was a low-key affair throughout, a meagre crowd of 8,000 in the 27,000-capacity ground.

Frank McDougall made his first European appearance for the Dons.

Aberdeen:
Leighton, McKimmie, Mitchell, Stark, McLeish, Miller, Weir, Simpson, McDougall, Cooper, Hewitt.
Subs: Angus for Stark, Gray for Weir.

Sunday 27 October 1985   **Skol League Cup final**
Aberdeen 3 Hibs 0   **Crowd 40,065**

The Dons win the Skol/League Cup for the first time in nine years. And for the first time in seven years of Ferguson's managership. Interesting to note Aberdeen did not lose a single goal during the competition. John Hewitt made his 250th first-team appearance for Aberdeen. On the game itself the Dons scored their first goal in the 9th minute when a clever reverse pass by McDougall found Hewitt and the Aberdeen striker broke through between two Hibs defenders, rounded the Hibs keeper and then chipped the ball back from the bye-line for **Black** to head it into the net.

Aberdeen were two up in 12 minutes and Hewitt was again involved in the build-up to the goal. This time his right-footed cross from the left found the head of **Stark** and was guided into the net.

With Aberdeen playing relaxed football it brought them a third goal in 62 minutes. Simpson broke through on the left and his cross-cum-shot reached **Black**, who turned the ball over the line.

Aberdeen:
Leighton, McKimmie, Mitchell, Stark, McLeish, Miller, Black,
Simpson, McDougall, Cooper, Hewitt.
Sub: Gray for Black.

Wednesday 30 October 1985   **Premier League**
Hearts 1 Aberdeen 0   **Crowd 12,446**

Hearts score their first league victory over the Dons in seven
years—with the only goal of the game coming in the 15th
minute. When Hearts won a corner, Leighton misjudged and
Levein found the net with a dipping header.

Aberdeen:
Leighton, McKimmie, Angus, Gray, McLeish, Miller, Weir,
Simpson, McDougall, Cooper, Hewitt.
Subs: Bett for Angus, Wright for McDougall.
Footnote: Dons sign striker Tommy Walker from Campsie Black
Watch.

Saturday 2 November 1985   **Premier League**
Aberdeen 4 Celtic 1   **Crowd 23,000**

Frank McDougall opened the scoring for the Dons with a header
in the 27th minute, then almost on the interval Provan equalised
with a brilliant swerving free-kick.

At the start of the second half McLeish sent the Celtic keeper
the wrong way and **McDougall** swooped in for his second, again
from a header.

In the 55th minute the Dons raced upfield once more for the
kill, Bett laying on the pass for the unmarked **McDougall.**

McDougall reserved his best goal for the last, scoring superbly
with a volley that gave the Celtic keeper absolutely no chance.

Aberdeen:
Leighton, McKimmie, Mitchell, Stark, McLeish, Miller, Black,
Simpson, McDougall, Cooper, Hewitt.
Subs: Wright for Hewitt, Bett for Stark.
Footnote: The last Dons player to score 4 goals against Celtic was
George Hamilton at Parkhead on 2 January 1947—Dons won 5-1.
Tony Harris scored the other goal.

Wednesday 6 November 1985   European Cup, 2nd round, 2nd leg
Aberdeen 1 Servette 0   **Crowd 19,000**

Frank McDougall scored his first European goal for the Dons but it was all that was required to put the Dons through to the next round of the European Cup.

The goal came in the 23rd minute: a diagonal pass from Cooper saw the ball bounce away from Weir, but he retrieved the situation magnificently and cut back to send in a right-foot cross which McDougall converted with a diving header past the Servette keeper.

Aberdeen:
Leighton, McKimmie, Weir, Stark, McLeish, Miller, Bett, Simpson, McDougall, Cooper, Hewitt.
Subs: Mitchell for Stark, Gray for Hewitt.
Footnote: Former Don Mark McGhee signs for Celtic from SV Hamburg for a fee in the region of £200,000. And former Don Doug Rougvie puts in a transfer request to Chelsea.

Saturday 9 November 1985   **Premier League**
Aberdeen 4 Dundee 1   **Crowd 12,000**

Dundee took the lead in the 6th minute with a Stephen goal. Aberdeen equalised out of the blue in the 21st minute. Jim Bett picked up a Steve Gray corner well outside the Dundee area before backheeling to Willie Miller who sent in a superb cross which **McLeish** headed powerfully into the net.

In the 67th minute Aberdeen went in the lead when **McDougall** collected a Weir corner on the half volley and smashed a tremendous drive into the net from 15 yards.

Billy Stark scored a third goal in the 83rd minute and the midfielder added yet another with a second header, this time from a Gray cross three minutes from time.

Aberdeen:
Leighton, McKimmie, Mitchell, Stark, McLeish, Miller, Gray, Bett, McDougall, Angus, Weir.
Sub: Falconer for Angus.

Saturday 16 November 1985   **Premier League**
Motherwell 1 Aberdeen 1   **Crowd 4,960**

Motherwell opened the scoring in the 21st minute when they were awarded a penalty after Alex McLeish had punched the ball clear.

The Dons equaliser also came from a penalty in which **Frank McDougall** did the business from the spot. This was in the 58th minute.

Aberdeen:

Leighton, McKimmie, Mitchell, Stark, McLeish, Miller, Gray, Simpson, McDougall, Bett, Weir.
Subs: Angus for Mitchell, Hewitt for Gray.
Footnote: Alex Ferguson has his first book published called *A Light in the North.*

Saturday 23 November 1985   **Premier League**
St. Mirren 1 Aberdeen 0   **Crowd 5,630**

A goal by Rooney in the 44th minute was all that was required to rob the Dons of the points.

Aberdeen:

Leighton, McKimmie, Mitchell, Stark, McLeish, Miller, Hewitt, Simpson, McDougall, Cooper, Weir.
Subs: McQueen for Mitchell, Angus for Hewitt.

Wednesday 11 December 1985   **Premier League**
Clydebank 2 Aberdeen 1   **Crowd 2,095**

Clydebank took a shock 8th minute lead. Hughes sent a 25-yard free-kick off the crossbar with Leighton at full stretch, and Larnach was all alone as he headed the rebound home with the keeper stranded.

The Dons were set back on their heels in 53 minutes when the battling Bankies went further ahead.

The Dons pulled one back in the 60th minute. Falconer swept a long ball wide to the right for the darting Miller to hook back across goal and **Black** headed past the helpless Gallacher.

Aberdeen:
Leighton, McKimmie, Mitchell, Stark, McLeish, Angus, Black,
Simpson, J. Miller, Cooper, Falconer.
Subs: Weir for Mitchell, McDougall for Falconer.
Footnote: 2 December, Alex Ferguson turns down offer to manage
Inter Milan. 4 December, Scotland drew 0-0 with Australia in
Melbourne in World Cup decider match. The following Aberdeen
players were in the Scotland team; Leighton, McLeish, Miller. Neale
Cooper was on the subs bench.

Saturday 14 December 1985   **Premier League**
Aberdeen 4 Hibs 0   **Crowd 11,500**

The Dons opened the scoring in the 18th minute. Mitchell sent in a
25-yarder and although it was straight at the Hibs keeper he could
not hold it, something **Angus** anticipated as he nipped in to net the
rebound.

The Dons second goal came after Joe Miller cut the ball back to
Weir. His first shot was blocked but Peter threaded the rebound
through a wall of green and white bodies to score. Weir was in full
flow by this time. He swung over a corner three minutes from the
end which broke to **Joe Miller** who scored with a swerving shot
confidently taken with the outside of his foot to put the Dons three
up.

In injury time **Alex McLeish** rose high to head in at the far post
following a corner.

Aberdeen:
Gunn, McKimmie, Mitchell, Stark, McLeish, Cooper, Black,
Simpson, McDougall, Angus, J. Miller.
Sub: Weir for Stark.

Saturday 21 December 1985   **Premier League**
Dundee United 2 Aberdeen 1   **Crowd 10,085**

Dundee United took the lead in the 9th minute with a Bannon
penalty. The Dons equalised in the 29th minute when Joe Miller
sent over a grounder from the right, Eric Black dummied and **Billy
Stark** cracked in a grounder from the edge of the box.

Paul Sturrock scored the winner for United in the 40th minute.

Aberdeen:
Leighton, McKimmie, Mitchell, Stark, McLeish, W. Miller, Black,
Angus, McDougall, Cooper, J. Miller.
Subs: Weir for McDougall, McQueen for Cooper.
Footnote: It is now 12 weeks since the Dons won a game outside
Pittodrie.

Wednesday 1 January 1986   **Premier League**
Dundee 0 Aberdeen 0   **Crowd 9,100**

As a result of this no scoring draw latest league placings are Hearts
28 points, 22 games; Aberdeen 24 points, 20 games; Dundee United
and Celtic 24 points, both having only played 19 games.

Aberdeen:
Leighton, McKimmie, McQueen, Stark, McLeish, Miller, Black,
Gray, Falconer, Cooper, J. Miller.
Subs: Angus for Gray, Wright for Falconer.

Saturday 4 January 1986   **Premier League**
Aberdeen 3 St. Mirren 1   **Crowd 11,500**

The Dons opened the scoring in 90 seconds. Neale Cooper picked
out Weir with a searching crossfield ball and Weir headed it back to
Joe Miller. The young striker's effort from close range was blocked,
but the ball rebounded to **Eric Black** who slammed the shot into the
empty net.

In the 19th minute, Bett sent Joe Miller off and running with a
pass up the left wing. A defender appeared to have cleared the
danger by getting to the ball first, but his passback to the keeper was
brilliantly intercepted by **Black**, who scored from a difficult angle.

St. Mirren scored from close range in the 55th minute. However
three minutes later the Dons made it 3-1. Black crossed in from the
left, Joe Miller touched the ball back to **Weir** who stroked it past the
St. Mirren keeper with some ease.

Aberdeen:
Leighton, Cooper, McQueen, Stark, McLeish, Miller, Black, Gray, J.
Miller, Bett, Weir.
Sub: Falconer for Gray.

Saturday 11 January 1986   **Premier League**
Celtic 1 Aberdeen 1   **Crowd 31,305**

In the 14th minute Jim Bett flighted forward a speculative pass which only **Joe Miller** went for; the Celtic keeper blocked his first effort, but young Miller slotted the rebound over the line.

In the 19th minute Celtic equalised with a Peter Grant goal.

Aberdeen:
Leighton, McKimmie, McQueen, Bett, McLeish, W. Miller, Black, Simpson, J. Miller, Cooper, Weir.
Subs: McDougall for J. Miller, Stark for Weir.

Saturday 18 January 1986   **Premier League**
Aberdeen 0 Hearts 1   **Crowd 21,500**

One goal was all that was required to give Hearts both points—the goal coming from John Colquhoun in the 83rd minute.

Interesting to note—the last time Hearts won at Pittodrie they ended up getting relegated, this year however their win stretches their unbeaten run to 17 games. They also become the first team to beat the Dons at Pittodrie in 13 months.

Aberdeen:
Leighton, McKimmie, McQueen, Stark, McLeish, W. Miller, Black, Simpson, McDougall, Bett, Weir.
Subs: J. Miller for McDougall, Mitchell for McQueen.
Footnote: Ex-Don Charlie Elvin signs for Berwick Rangers.

Saturday 1 February 1986   **Premier League**
Rangers 1 Aberdeen 1   **Crowd 29,887**

The Dons went ahead in the 3rd minute. Tommy McQueen took a quick throw-in down the right to Peter Weir who swung the ball into the middle. **Joe Miller** in complete isolation leaped and headed a beauty into the back of the net.

Rangers equalised in the 52nd minute from a Hugh Burns shot from 7 metres.

Aberdeen:
Leighton, McQueen, Stark, McKimmie, McLeish, W. Miller, Black,

Simpson, J. Miller, Bett, Weir.
Sub: Mitchell for McQueen.
Footnote: Aberdeen have not won a game outside Pittodrie since September 28 1985—and that was at Ibrox.

Wednesday 5 February 1986   **Scottish Cup 3rd round**
Aberdeen 4 Montrose 1   **Crowd 9,000**

Aberdeen opened the scoring in the 27th minute following a Weir corner kick which reached Miller, waiting wide on the right. Miller's cross was headed into the corner of the net by **Stark.**

With the second half only two minutes old Aberdeen increased their lead. McLeish rose in the goalmouth to knock a Bett corner kick out to the right and **Miller** was waiting to hammer a low shot into the far corner of the net.

A McQueen tackle on a Montrose defender resulted in a spot kick for the visitors, who scored from the spot in the 56th minute.

Aberdeen went 3-1 up in the 74th minute. Black touched a Miller free kick neatly into the path of **McDougall**, who controlled the ball on the move before slipping it wide of the keeper as he came out.

In the 81st minute **McLeish** got his head to a Bett flag kick and netted from close range, to make the final score 4-1 in favour of the Dons.

Aberdeen:
Leighton, McKimmie, McQueen, Stark, McLeish, Miller, Black, Simpson, McDougall, Bett, Weir.
Sub: Porteous for Weir.
Footnote: This was the first time that the two clubs had met in a Scottish Cup tie.

Saturday 8 February 1986   **Premier League**
Aberdeen 4 Clydebank 1   **Crowd 11,000**

Aberdeen went ahead in the 15th minute. McDougall was clean through from a nice Stark-Joe Miller move, but was brought down by the keeper **Jim Bett** scored from the spot.

The Dons went two up in the 29th minute. **Eric Black** rose like a rocket from its pad to blast a Willie Miller cross into the net.

Five minutes later **Black** was in a dandy position to take advantage of a McDougall dummy and head home his second goal.

Eric Black completed his hat-trick in the 53rd minute following a courageous cross from the right by Stark which found Black perfectly placed at the far post to head home the Dons' fourth goal.

Clydebank scored a consolation goal in the 88th minute.

Aberdeen:
Leighton, McKimmie, Angus, Stark, McLeish, W. Miller, Black, Simpson, McDougall, Bett, J. Miller.
Subs: Porteous for Stark, Mitchell for Simpson.

Saturday 15 February 1986   **Scottish Cup 4th round**
Arbroath 0 Aberdeen 1   **Crowd 6,017**

The only goal of the game came in the 47th minute. Cooper sent over a crafty cross from the right and **Joe Miller** showed great composure in dragging the ball down, keeping it under control, then beating the keeper with a perfect low drive.

Aberdeen:
Leighton, Cooper, McQueen, Bett, McLeish, Miller, Black, Simpson, McDougall, Angus, J. Miller.
Subs: not used.
Footnote: The Dons last met Arbroath in a Scottish Cup game in season 1979/78, which was a third round tie at Gayfield. The Dons were held to a 1-1 draw. However in the replay at Pittodrie the Dons had little difficulty in beating Arbroath 5-0.

Wednesday 19 February 1986   **Premier League**
Aberdeen 1 Rangers 0   **Crowd 18,700**

Aberdeen needed only one goal to get both points—the goal coming in the 67th minute. Joe Miller started the move with a break through the middle before squaring the ball to Simpson, who in turn slipped it into the path of **Angus**, who hit a left foot drive into the net from 20 yards.

Aberdeen:
Leighton, McKimmie, McQueen, Cooper, McLeish, W. Miller,

Black, Simpson, McDougall, Bett, J. Miller.
Subs: Angus for McQueen, Wright for McDougall.

Saturday 22 February 1986   **Premier League**
Hibs 0 Aberdeen 1   **Crowd 9,500**

A 13th minute goal from **Paul Wright** was the only goal of the
game. Alex McLeish sent a long ball into the Hibs area, Gordon Rae
appeared to stumble, and Wright controlled the ball superbly before
crashing it into the net from 12 yards.

Aberdeen:
Leighton, McKimmie, Angus, Stark, McLeish, W. Miller, Black,
Simpson, Wright, Cooper, J. Miller.
Subs: Mitchell for Stark, Hewitt for J. Miller.
Footnote: Aberdeen sign 16-year-old striker Archie McGeachie from
Rangers Boys Club.

Wednesday 5 March 1986   European Cup, quarter-final, 1st leg
Aberdeen 2 IFK Gothenburg 2   **Crowd 20,000**

Aberdeen opened the scoring in the 16th minute: a Cooper cross
from the right found McLeish in the middle and he neatly turned
the ball into the path of **Willie Miller** who cracked a left foot shot on
the run into the roof of the net from 15 yards.

Gothenburg equalised in the 42nd minute—when a cross found
Tord Holmgren unmarked in the middle and he sent the ball just
inside the top of Gunn's right-hand upright.

In the 79th minute a long clearance by Gunn was missed by a
Gothenburg defender. **Hewitt** ran in to slide the ball past the
advancing keeper.

Disaster for the Dons as Gothenburg equalised in the last
minute.

Aberdeen:
Gunn, Cooper, Angus, Stark, McLeish, W. Miller, Black, Simpson,
J. Miller, Bett, Weir.
Subs: Hewitt for J. Miller, McKimmie for Simpson.
Footnote: Willie Miller also makes his 50th European appearance for

the Dons while Bryan Gunn makes his first European appearance for the Dons.

Saturday 8 March 1986   **Scottish Cup quarter-final**
Dundee 2 Aberdeen 2   **Crowd 13,188**

The Dons opened the scoring in the 24th minute. Eric Black's long and accurate pass landed right on **Hewitt's** head, leaving the Dundee keeper with no chance.

Two minutes later Dundee equalised when they took off on the left with Mennie and Brown involved before Harvey put the ball in the back of the net.

Dundee went into the lead following a corner. The cross from Connor was knocked on by Smith for Brown to get the final touch.

Aberdeen's equaliser came in the 73rd minute when Jim Duffy tried a simple passback. The Dundee keeper was too casual and failed to gather the ball. That allowed Neil Simpson to whip in a cross from which **John Hewitt** hit his second goal.

Aberdeen:
Leighton, McKimmie, McLeish, Miller, Angus, Bett, Cooper, Simpson, Black, Hewitt, Weir.
Subs: Stark for Angus, Wright for Weir.
Footnote: The last time Aberdeen and Dundee drew in a Scottish Cup game was on 16 February 1977 at Dens Park where the game ended in a 0-0 draw. Dundee went on to win the replay at Pittodrie 2-1.

Wednesday 12 March 1986 **Scottish Cup quarter-final (replay)**
Aberdeen 2 Dundee 1 (after extra time)   **Crowd 20,412**

Dundee took the lead in the 19th minute. Leighton punched out a McKinley cross from the left but Stephen gathered the ball and sent it into the net from 15 yards.

In the 38th minute **Eric Black** met a lobbed cross from McKimmie and headed the ball well out of the reach of the Dundee keeper.

With the game still tied at the end of full-time, the Dons scored the winning goal in the 11th minute of extra time when **Weir** sent in a cross from the left and the ball floated over the Dundee keeper and under the crossbar.

Aberdeen:

Leighton, Cooper, McKimmie, Stark, McLeish, Miller, Black, Simpson, Hewitt, Bett, Weir.

Subs: Angus for Stark, Wright for Black.

Saturday 15 March 1986   **Premier League**
St. Mirren 1 Aberdeen 1   **Crowd 4,448**

In 22 minutes St. Mirren raced ahead when Clark completed a run initiated by an Abercrombie free-kick, and finished with a great right foot shot that left Leighton helpless.

Aberdeen got the equaliser via a **Willie Miller** try that went in off the woodwork in the 33rd minute.

Aberdeen:

Leighton, McKimmie, McQueen, Cooper, McLeish, W. Miller, J. Miller, Angus, Wright, Bett, Hewitt.

Subs: Stark for McQueen, Porteous for J. Miller.

Wednesday 19 March 1986 European Cup quarter-final, 2nd leg
IFK Gothenburg 0 Aberdeen 0 (aggregate 2-2)   Crowd 44,400

Aberdeen go out of the European Cup on the away goal rule—Aberdeen also go out of the competition without losing a game.

Aberdeen:

Leighton, McKimmie, Mitchell, Cooper, McLeish, Miller, Black, Angus, Hewitt, Bett, Weir.

Subs: Stark for Mitchell, McDougall for Black.

Saturday 22 March 1986   **Premier League**
Aberdeen 0 Dundee 0   **Crowd 13,000**

Aberdeen's championship challenge was blown off course when Dundee took away a valuable point with both teams failing to find the net.

Aberdeen:
Leighton, McKimmie, Angus, Cooper, McLeish, W. Miller, J. Miller,
Stark, Wright, Bett, Hewitt.
Subs: Mitchell for Wright, Falconer for Hewitt.

Saturday 29 March 1986   **Premier League**
Motherwell 0 Aberdeen 1   **Crowd 4,597**

Stand-in keeper Bryan Gunn had a big hand in Aberdeen's first
Premier League win in five weeks.

The goal that won the points came in the 7th minute when
Motherwell could not get the ball out of the danger zone. Joe Miller
slipped the ball through to **Hewitt** who tucked the ball past the
Motherwell keeper.

Aberdeen:
Gunn, McKimmie, McQueen, Stark, Cooper, W. Miller, J. Miller,
Angus, Hewitt, Bett, McMaster.
Sub: Gray for J. Miller.

Saturday 5 April 1986   **Scottish Cup semi-final**
Aberdeen 3 Hibs 0   **Crowd 19,165**

Aberdeen took the lead in 19 minutes through a skilfully worked
goal which left the Hibs rearguard looking pedestrian. Black hooked
on an Angus throw-in into the goalmouth where McDougall
dummied, leaving **Stark** with time and room to place his header past
Rough from five yards.

The Dons went two up in the 35th minute when Hewitt held off
three Hibs defenders on the left flank to deliver a perfect cross to
the far post where **Eric Black** made no mistake with a header.

Aberdeen's third goal came in the 85th minute—McMaster
passed to Hewitt on the left and the winger outpaced Sneddon to
cross into the goalmouth where **Joe Miller** headed powerfully past
the Hibs keeper.

Aberdeen:
Gunn, McKimmie, Angus, Stark, McLeish, W. Miller, Black,

Cooper, McDougall, Bett, Hewitt.
Subs: McMaster for Stark, J. Miller for Cooper.
Footnote: Aberdeen have played 17 cup ties this season without defeat.

Wednesday 9 April 1986	**Premier League**
Aberdeen 3 Motherwell 2	**Crowd 10,300**

It took Aberdeen only 90 seconds to get into the lead. Black was impeded by Murray just outside the corner of the Motherwell penalty box. Willie Miller dummied to take the free-kick and McMaster rolled the ball square across the front of the box where it was met by **Bett** whose raging shot left the Motherwell keeper helpless.

Aberdeen went two up in the 35th minute. Gray sent a short corner to Weir out on the right and he sent over a left foot cross which was met at the near post by Black, who back-headed the ball for **McDougall** to head it into the net at the far post.

Motherwell shocked the Dons by getting a goal three minutes later. A gap was found in the Aberdeen defence and Reilly hit a shot on the turn to direct the ball past Gunn.

Motherwell equalised through Kennedy in the 76th minute but Aberdeen got the winning goal five minutes later. A McLeish free-kick from his own half was back-headed by Black and **Weir** dashed into the goalmouth to dispatch the ball into the net.

Aberdeen:

Gunn, McKimmie, McQueen, McMaster, McLeish, W. Miller, Black, Gray, McDougall, Bett, Weir.
Subs: McIntyre for McMaster, J. Miller for McDougall.
Footnote: Rangers sack Jock Wallace and appoint Graeme Souness as their new manager. Former Don Dom Sullivan takes over as manager of Alloa Athletic.

Saturday 12 April 1986	**Premier League**
Aberdeen 0 Celtic 1	**Crowd 22,000**

A Mo Johnstone goal in the 49th minute was enough to give Celtic both points.

Aberdeen:

Gunn, McKimmie, McQueen, Stark, McLeish, W. Miller, Black, Mitchell, J. Miller, Bett, Hewitt.

Subs: McMaster for McQueen, Falconer for Hewitt.

Wednesday 16 April 1986   Premier League
Aberdeen 0 Dundee United 1   Crowd 8,500

The chances of Aberdeen winning the Premier League championship took a step back following a 26th minute Richard Gough goal which was all that was required to give Dundee United both points.

Aberdeen:

Gunn, McKimmie, Mitchell, Robertson, McLeish, W. Miller, Black, Angus, J. Miller, Bett, Weir.

Subs: McMaster for Black, Porteous for Angus.

Sunday 20 April 1986   Premier League
Hearts 1 Aberdeen 1   Crowd 19,047

Aberdeen went into the lead via a **Peter Weir** penalty goal, and it looked very much like the Dons would end Hearts unbeaten run of 29 games without defeat. However with three minutes still to go Colquhoun equalised giving Hearts a share of the points and increased their unbeaten run to 30 games.

Aberdeen:

Gunn, McKimmie, McQueen, McMaster, McLeish, W. Miller, Hewitt, Mitchell, J. Miller, Bett, Weir.

Subs: Black for Hewitt, I. Robertson for Mitchell.

Footnote: This was the very first League game to be televised live in Scotland.

Saturday 27 April 1986   Premier League
Aberdeen 1 Rangers 1   Crowd 17,000

Rangers went ahead in the 50th minute—following a move by McMinn from inside his own half. He proceeded to weave past the red jerseys and finally beat Gunn with a rising shot.

Hewitt equalised for the Dons in the 57th minute. Weir swung over a corner from the right and with the help of McLeish the ball found its way to Hewitt who hit a powerful shot from 16 yards into the back of the net.

Aberdeen:

Gunn, Mitchell, McIntyre, McMaster, McLeish, W. Miller, Gray, Robertson, J. Miller, Hewitt, Weir.
Subs: Wright for McIntyre, Porteous for Mitchell.

Saturday 3 May 1986   **Premier League**
Clydebank 0 Aberdeen 6   **Crowd 2,383**

The Dons reserved their highest league win of the season till the last game where they ran out easy winners.

The Dons went ahead in nine minutes—from a corner, a Peter Weir inswinger from the right, **Billy Stark** rose and head-flicked the ball in at the post.

A minute later the Dons went two up. **McMaster** had a go from outside the box and he powered the ball past the Clydebank keeper.

Peter Weir put the Dons three up in the 16th minute as Clydebank failed to clear a cross. Weir picked up the ball and hammered a beauty into the back of the net.

The Dons went four up in the 29th minute when McMaster stroked the ball into the path of **John Hewitt** who struck the ball home from 15 yards.

Goal number five came in the 38th minute. Weir and Stark combined for the latter to cross low to **Frank McDougall** who fired the ball into the net.

McDougall put the Dons six up in the 67th minute when Clydebank failed to clear a Hewitt cross.

Aberdeen:

Gunn, McKimmie, McQueen, Stark, Irvine, McIntyre, Gray, Hewitt, McDougall, McMaster, Weir.
Subs: Porteous for Gray, Robertson for McMaster.
Footnote: Brian Irvine made his first Premier appearance for the Dons. Dundee ended Hearts run of 31 games without a defeat with

their 2-0 win at Dens Park. Celtic by beating St. Mirren 5-0 become the Premier League Champions 1985/86.

Saturday 10 May 1986	**Scottish Cup Final**
Aberdeen 3 Hearts 0	**Crowd 62,841**

In the 101st Scottish Cup final Aberdeen lifted the Scottish Cup for the fourth time in five years.

Aberdeen took the lead in the fifth minute. Willie Miller set the ball rolling with a long accurate pass to **John Hewitt** who pulled down the ball, turned and made ground towards the defenders and then rapped a left-footer into the corner of the net from the edge of the box.

Goal number two came in the 48th minute. Peter Weir skimmed past Kidd on the left flank before powering a low ball into the penalty area. McDougall ran over the ball and there was **Hewitt** to ram the ball home.

In the 74th minute Aberdeen went three up when **Billy Stark** headed a Peter Weir free-kick and gave the Hearts keeper no chance.

Aberdeen:
Leighton, McKimmie, McQueen, McMaster, McLeish, Miller, Hewitt, Cooper, McDougall, Bett, Weir.
Subs: Stark for McMaster, J. Miller for Hewitt.
Footnote: In the Premier League games played at Pittodrie, season 1985/86, a total of 257,871 came through the turnstiles which represents a drop of 27,915 from season 1984/85. Eric Black moves to French Club Metz under freedom of contract, Eric was signed on an S form while still at Alness Academy in 1980. He made 215 first-team appearances including 38 as a substitute. He scored 79 first-team goals.

Aberdeen FC Statistics
1985/86

PREMIER LEAGUE

P	W	D	L	F	A	Pts	Psn
36	16	12	8	62	31	44	4th

Goal scorers. Premier League games only.

McDougall	14	Bett	3
Black	8	Angus	2
Stark	8	Wright	2
Hewitt	6	W. Miller	1
Weir	5	Simpson	1
J. Miller	3	McQueen	1
McKimmie	3	Gray	1
McLeish	3	McMaster	1

Appearances (subs in brackets). Premier League games only.

McKimmie	34(–)	J. Miller	17(2)
McLeish	34(–)	McQueen	15(2)
W. Miller	33(–)	Angus	12(5)
Stark	28(2)	Gray	10(3)
Leighton	26(–)	Gunn	10(–)
Black	23(3)	McMaster	5(2)
McDougall	22(3)	Wright	3(7)
Bett	22(2)	Falconer	2(6)
Simpson	22(–)	McIntyre	2(3)
Cooper	20(3)	Robertson	2(2)
Hewitt	18(5)	Irvine	1(–)
Mitchell	18(5)	Porteous	0(6)
Weir	17(4)		

EUROPEAN CUP

P	W	D	L	F	A
6	3	3	0	10	4

Goal scorers

Hewitt	3	Falconer	1
Black	1	Simpson	1
Stark	1	McDougall	1
Gray	1	W. Miller	1

Appearances (subs in brackets). European Cup games only.

McLeish	6(–)	Simpson	4(–)
W. Miller	6(–)	Mitchell	3(2)
Cooper	6(–)	Gray	2(2)
McKimmie	5(1)	Angus	2(2)
Hewitt	5(1)	McDougall	2(1)
Leighton	5(–)	Wright	1(1)
Stark	4(1)	McQueen	1(–)
Black	4(–)	J Miller	1(–)
Bett	4(–)	Gunn	1(–)
Weir	4(–)	Falconer	0(1)

SKOL LEAGUE CUP

P	W	D	L	F	A
6	6	0	0	13	0

Goal scorers

McDougall	4	McQueen	1
Black	4	Hewitt	1
Stark	3		

Appearances (subs in brackets). Skol League Cup games only.

McLeish	6(–)	Black	3(1)
Miller	6(–)	Cooper	3(1)
Hewitt	6(–)	Bett	3(–)
Simpson	6(–)	Weir	3(–)
McKimmie	6(–)	Gunn	2(–)
McDougall	6(–)	McQueen	2(–)
Stark	5(1)	Gray	1(3)
Leighton	4(–)	Angus	1(–)
Mitchell	4(–)	Falconer	0(1)

SCOTTISH CUP

P	W	D	L	F	A
6	5	1	0	15	4

Goal scorers

Hewitt	4	W. Miller	1
Stark	3	McDougall	1
Black	2	McLeish	1
J. Miller	2	Weir	1

Appearances (subs in brackets). Scottish Cup games only.

McLeish	6(–)	Hewitt	4(–)
W. Miller	6(–)	Stark	3(2)
Bett	6(–)	Angus	3(1)
Leighton	5(–)	McQueen	3(–)
McKimmie	5(–)	J. Miller	1(2)
Black	5(–)	McMaster	1(1)
Cooper	5(–)	Gunn	1(–)
Simpson	4(–)	Wright	0(2)
McDougall	4(–)	Porteous	0(1)
Weir	4(–)		

	P	W	D	L	F	A
Scottish Cup	6	5	1	0	15	4
European Cup	6	3	3	0	10	4
Premier League	36	16	12	8	62	31
Skol/League Cup	6	6	0	0	13	0
	54	30	16	8	100	39

GOAL SCORERS
LEAGUE and CUP GAMES

	P/L	SL/C	S/C	E/C	Total
F. McDougall	14	4	1	1	20
E. Black	8	4	2	1	15
B. Stark	8	3	3	1	15
J. Hewitt	6	1	4	3	14
P. Weir	5	0	1	0	6
J. Miller	3	0	2	0	5
A. McLeish	3	0	1	0	4
S. McKimmie	3	0	0	0	3
J. Bett	3	0	0	0	3
W. Miller	1	0	1	1	3
I. Angus	2	0	0	0	2
P. Wright	2	0	0	0	2
N. Simpson	1	0	0	1	2
T. McQueen	1	1	0	0	2
S. Gray	1	0	0	1	2
J. McMaster	1	0	0	0	1
W. Falconer	0	0	0	1	1

APPEARANCES
LEAGUE & CUP GAMES

	P/L	E/C	SL/C	S/C	Total
A. McLeish	34	6	6	6	52
W. Miller	33	6	6	6	51
S. McKimmie	34	5(1)	6	5	50(1)
B. Stark	28(2)	4(1)	5(1)	3(2)	40(6)
J. Leighton	26	5	4	5	40
N. Simpson	22	4	6	4	36
E. Black	23(3)	4	3(1)	5	35(4)
J. Bett	22(2)	4	3	6	35(2)
F. McDougall	22(3)	2(1)	6	4	34(4)
N. Cooper	20(3)	6	3(1)	5	34(4)
J. Hewitt	18(5)	5(1)	6	4	33(6)
P. Weir	17(4)	4	3	4	28(4)
B. Mitchell	18(5)	3(2)	4	0	25(7)
T. McQueen	15(2)	1	2	3	21(2)
I. Angus	12(5)	2(2)	1	3(1)	18(8)
J. Miller	17(2)	1	0	1(2)	19(4)
B. Gunn	10	1	2	1	14
S. Gray	10(3)	2(2)	1(3)	0	13(8)
J. McMaster	5(2)	0	0	1(1)	6(3)
P. Wright	3(7)	1(1)	0	0(2)	4(10)
W. Falconer	2(6)	0(1)	0(1)	0	2(8)
T. McIntyre	2(3)	0	0	0	2(3)
I. Robertson	2(2)	0	0	0	2(2)
B. Irvine	1	0	0	0	1
I. Porteous	0	0	0	0(1)	0(1)

Additional News
The whole of Scottish Football was saddened by the death of
Aberdeen Vice-Chairman Chris Anderson in June 1986—Mr
Anderson was 61. Mr Anderson signed for the Dons as a player
from Junior side Muggiemoss in 1943—and made 103 first-team
appearances for the Dons before ending his playing career with
Arbroath.

He rejoined Aberdeen FC as a director in 1967 and in 1970 he
became the Club's Vice-Chairman. In 1981 he was awarded the
OBE for his services to Scottish Sport. As a tribute to Chris
Anderson, Linksfield Stadium is to be given a facelift and
renamed **The Chris Anderson Memorial Stadium.**

Former Assistant manager Archie Knox, who left Aberdeen FC
two and a half years ago to become manager of Dundee—is
appointed co-manager of Aberdeen FC.

Neale Cooper moves from Pittodrie under freedom of contract to
Aston Villa. Born in India, Neale has been at Pittodrie since being
a ball boy at 10 and became Aberdeen's youngest S signing while
he was a pupil of Hazlehead Academy—he went on to make 245
first-team appearances including 30 as sub.

In August 1986 Aberdeen signed Dundee mid-field player Robert
Connor from Dundee in a £350,000 transfer deal which included
the departure of Ian Angus to Dens Park.

Now You Know . . .

At a match between Newcastle United and Portsmouth on 5 December 1931 their were no goals—OR CORNER KICKS.

Aston Villa centre-half Chris Nicholl scored all four goals in a 2-2 result v Leicester City on 20 March 1976. Twice he put Leicester in front with own goals then equalised for Villa.

Liverpool used only 14 players in 42 matches when they won the Football League championship in season 1965/66.

In season 1925/26 Cardiff City had a record 17 internationals on their playing staff—9 Welsh, 4 Scottish and 4 Irish.

In 1949 Rangers became the first Scottish team to win League, League Cup and Scottish Cup in the same season.

The Scottish Cup tie between Inverness Thistle and Falkirk during the winter of 1978/79 was postponed a record 29 times due to weather conditions. Falkirk eventually won 4-0.